LONDON'S forgotten CHILDREN

ABOUT THE AUTHOR

Gillian Pugh was chief executive of Coram from 1997–2005. She has advised governments in this country and overseas on services for children and families, and has published widely on early years and primary education, parental support, and joined up approaches to working with children, as well as a local history of her village in Hertfordshire. Before her retirement, she was visiting professor at the Institute of Education in London and chair of the National Children's Bureau. In retirement she chairs her local educational trust, and enjoys spending time with her eight grandchildren, singing, walking and gardening. She was created a Dame in 2005 for services to children and families.

LONDON'S
forgotten
CHILDREN

THOMAS CORAM AND
THE FOUNDLING HOSPITAL

GILLIAN PUGH

The
History
Press

First published 2007
Reprinted 2008, 2013
This revised paperback edition first published 2022

The History Press
97 St George's Place, Cheltenham,
Gloucestershire, GL50 3QB
www.thehistorypress.co.uk

ISBN 978 1 80399 187 0

Typesetting and origination by The History Press
Printed and bound in Great Britain by TJ Books Limited, Padstow, Cornwall.

Trees for LYfe

CONTENTS

Acknowledgements

My interest in writing this book began well before I joined the Thomas Coram Foundation for Children – as it was then called – as chief executive in 1997. I had long been interested in both the children's charity and its current work and past history, and in the historic picture collection for which, when I joined the organisation, I was also responsible.

My knowledge and understanding of the fascinating history of the organisation grew during the eight years at Coram, but it was not until I retired that I had time to do the further research that was required to put this book together. It has been a fascinating journey.

Many people have helped me in my quest to tell, for the first time, the history of the Foundling Hospital from the 1730s to the present day. I have drawn heavily on a number of key sources, particularly Ruth McClure's *Coram's Children: The London Foundling Hospital in the Eighteenth Century*; Gillian Wagner's *Thomas Coram,*

Gent, two books by my predecessors as senior officers of the organisation – John Brownlow's *Memoranda, or Chronicle of the Foundling Hospital* published in 1847 and R.H Nichols and F.A Wray's detailed *History of the Foundling Hospital* published in 1935 and a selection from the huge number of documents (weighing an estimated 8 tonnes) in the London Metropolitan Archives.

One of the great pleasures of my time at Coram was meeting so many former pupils and members of the Old Coram Association. I am indebted to those who have shared their memories with me and with Virginia Makins, and to those who were also interviewed by Chris Oliver and Peter Aggleton for their study *Coram's Children: Growing up in the care of the Foundling Hospital 1900–1955.* I would particularly like to thank Harold Tarrant, John Caldicott, Lydia Carmichael, Mary Bentley and Jocelyn Gamble for their help and for permission to quote from their interviews and writings, Gillian Erskine for permission to quote from her late husband Tom's autobiography and the Old Coram Association for permission to quote from *Coram News.*

Current and former staff and governors of Coram Family and colleagues in the Foundling Museum have been generous with the information they have shared with me, and many have commented on earlier drafts of this book. A particular thank you to William Barnes, Dorothy Baulch, Peter Brown, Steve Hudd, Jeanne Kaniuk, Colin Masters, Val Molloy, Gordon Parker, Wendy Rose, Lonica Vanclay and Lorna Zumpe and to honorary archivists John Orr and Gillian Clark. Also to Janet Snook who worked in the Thomas Coram children's centre in the 1970s, to Bernadette Duffy who is the head of centre today, and to Sandy Wynn who runs Coram's Fields.

Thank you also to Jenny Bourne Taylor, Professor of English at Sussex University for sharing with me her material relating to Charles Dickens and John Brownlow in the nineteenth century; to Virginia Makins who interviewed many former pupils and gave me access to her notes; and to Nicola Hilliard at the National Children's Bureau for allowing me to follow up much of the historical material through the NCB library.

For permission to use photographs and help in finding and reproducing them, further thanks are due. To Coram Family for permission to reproduce the following which are in the care of the Foundling Museum and to Alison Duke from the Foundling Museum for her help in locating the images: portrait of *Captain Thomas Coram* and *Moses Brought Before Pharoahs Daughter* by Hogarth; portrait of *Captain Thomas Coram* by Nebot; the engraving of the Foundling Hospital; *Admission of children to the Hospital by ballot* by Wale; *The Foundling Hospital chapel* and *Girls dining room* by Sanders; *A Foundling Boy* and *A Foundling Girl* by Copping; *The Foundling Hospital* by Wilson; photograph of the marble chimney by Rysbrack; the bust of Handel by Roubiliac; *The Finding of the Infant Moses in the Bulrushes* by Hayman; *The Foundling Restored to its Mother* and *The Christening* by Brownlow King; *Girls in the Chapel* by Anderson; and visitors watching children eat Sunday lunch from the *Illustrated London News*.

The March of the Guards to Finchley by Hogarth and the tokens are owned by the Foundling Museum; the photograph of the Court Room is by James Robinson; the painting of the Foundling Museum is by Ann Usborne and is reproduced by permission of Persephone Books.

The photographs of Coram's Fields are reproduced with permission of Sandy Wynn.

All other photographs are reproduced with the permission of Coram Family, with a particular thank you to Jocelyn Gamble for her help in reproducing photographs from the archives.

And finally thank you to Kate Adie for her interest in the work of the Foundling Hospital and the children who grew up in it, and for her Foreword to this book.

Gillian Pugh,
November 2006

Postscript

The opportunity to publish a revised edition of the book in 2022 has enabled me to update the work of Coram and the Foundling Museum and to examine new insights from the archives. My grateful thanks to Dr Carol Homden, Group Chief Executive of Coram and Caro Howell and Alison Duke of the Foundling Museum for their support in this task.

Gillian Pugh
September 2022

List of Illustrations

Mono Illustrations

1 Heading to the subscription roll designed by William Hogarth. © Coram Family.
2 *Captain Thomas Coram* by B. Nebot, 1741. © Coram Family in the care of the Foundling Museum.
3 Statue of Thomas Coram outside the Foundling Museum and Coram Family. © Coram Family in the care of the Foundling Museum.
4 Detail from a map of London by John Rocque, 1746. The site of the Foundling Hospital was north of the northern edge of London. © Coram Family.
5 *Admission of children to the Hospital by ballot* by Samuel Wale, 1749. © Coram Family in the care of the Foundling Museum.
6 *The Foundling Hospital chapel looking west* by John Sanders, 1773. Reproduced by permission of the Trustees of the William Salt Library.

7   Boys' dining room, photographed in the early 1900s. © Coram Family.

8   *Girls' dining room* by John Sanders, 1773, showing the Hogarth portrait of Thomas Coram hanging to the right of the picture. Reproduced by permission of the Trustees of the William Salt Library.

9   Boys' dormitory, west wing, photographed in the early 1900s. © Coram Family.

10 The marble mantelpiece in the Court Room – *Charity and children engaged in navigation and husbandry* – by John Michael Rysbrack, 1745. © Coram Family in the care of the Foundling Museum.

11 Terracotta bust of George Frideric Handel by Louis-Francois Roubiliac, 1739. © Coram Family in the care of the Foundling Museum.

12 Invitation to the first performance of *Messiah* by George Frideric Handel, 1 May 1750. © Coram Family.

13 Leaving certificate for apprentice Esther Mayhew, 1855. © Coram Family.

14 The boys' band, Foundling Hospital, early 1900s. © Coram Family.

15 Visitors watching children eat Sunday lunch, 1872. by J. Swain after H.T. Thomas, from *Illustrated London News* 7 December. © Coram Family in the care of the Foundling Museum.

16 The boys' school room, Foundling Hospital early 1900s. © Coram Family.

17 The girls' school room, Foundling Hospital, early 1900s. © Coram Family.

18 The infants' school room, Foundling Hospital, early 1900s. © Coram Family.

Colour Illustrations

FOREWORD

It seems strange that any child should be forgotten. However, there have always been familiar phrases which have hinted at children out of sight, out of mind: 'She's in trouble', 'there was a child, I believe', 'A boy – but the family doesn't talk about it.'

For centuries, a combination of social prejudice and religious disapproval effectively banished some children from the family tree. Unwanted, illegitimate, abandoned, victims of dire poverty, such children were seen as a problem to be tidied away. Across Europe there were 'turning wheels' in every major city, anonymous gateways to huge institutions which cloistered the unwanted. In America, the railroad sped hundreds of thousands of boys and girls, cut off from their origins, to a new life in the West, with strangers. In Russia, the Tsars personally endowed immense Foundling Hospitals, encouraging the idea that the State was a more reliable carer than the family.

Those who sought to deal with the social 'difficulty' of the abandoned were sometimes benevolent, sometimes filled with reforming zeal – for these were the offspring of unacceptable unions and often thought to be tainted by their parents' behaviour. The story in Britain has a touch of both influences, but centres on a true hero: Captain Thomas Coram, the creator of the Foundling Hospital in London.

The Coram story is the story of our attitude to children. And what makes it particularly poignant are the voices of those who were still in the Foundling Hospital within living memory – very much the heirs to a 200 year-old tradition – and still with us today.

It is a vitally important story, for we are now supposed to know so much more about the importance of childhood and the significance of the relationship between parent and child. The picture of gaunt and draughty buildings into which children used to be herded and disciplined according to the principles of the time fills us with dismay. However, although these institutions have disappeared, we are still grappling with problems within families and have no reason for complacency when confronted with the modern statistics for neglect and cruelty. (Even abandonment is still with us, a steady stream of foundlings every year left in bus shelters and doorways.)

We need to know how our attitudes to children have been shaped, and how much prejudice today stems from ancient ideas: mutterings such as 'bad blood will out' and 'the child conceived in sin' may sound Victorian (or more probably mediaeval), but they can still be heard in dark corners and live in the minds of those who are unwilling to see children as individuals at the mercy of circumstances. For an insight into what shapes our views, we have to reach back to the strong influences which religious teaching and economic necessity brought to bear on ordinary families. For centuries, legitimacy, inheritance, superstition, starvation and inequality swirled around a newborn child, with emotional well-being hardly registering. Hard to believe in today's world? No, not when you hear arguments grounded in social agendas, cultural heritage and material circumstances advanced at the expense of love and care.

The attitude of Church and State needs to be reviewed in light of the Coram experience: who should take over from parents who are unable to look after their children? Institutions, wet-nurses, fostering, orphanages, even transportation – all have been tried. Today there is still debate as to the best kind of care for those outside the conventional family, and the roots of that debate are well embedded in the Middle Ages. Understanding the consequences of what has been tried is essential to assessing new courses of action. Nor is it long since children ceased to be regarded as property, rather than small people. Even so, the rights of the child are still a subject of debate in many sensitive situations, and it is well worth understanding how much has changed in the past couple of centuries.

Thomas Coram had a good notion of what might be right for a child, but like many kind-hearted and modest men, he didn't carve his name prominently. He is remembered today in an open space in north London – Coram's Fields. However, his good intentions live on, for if you cross Coram's Fields – heading for the Foundling Museum – you will see a sign which is probably unique in the land: 'Adults not admitted unless accompanied by a child'. You may also hear children's voices, belonging to those who are being helped by Coram Family, the organisation which carries on the tradition of innovative action on behalf of today's 'forgotten children'.

This is a book about all such children, past and present – and if we care about any child's future, we need to read about the past and the tradition of Coram.

Kate Adie
Former BBC Chief News Correspondent and author of three best-selling books including *Nobody's Child: Who are you when you don't know your past?* (Hodder and Stoughton, 2005)

INTRODUCTION

The buzz in the room gets louder as more and more people arrive. The majority are men and women in their sixties and older, but a few have brought their grown-up children with them. Snatches of conversation suggest that these are people who know each other well and have done so for many years. Some are greeting people as though they are long-lost family. There are jokes about former teachers, and nicknames are banded about. There are quips about money lent and not returned, and old grievances are aired. Boxes of old school photos are laid out on a table and there is much reminiscing as these men and women catch sight of themselves in their earlier days.

It might be any school reunion, except that people keep telling you: 'This is my family'. For this is a meeting of the Old Coram Association, the former pupils of the London Foundling Hospital. Three times a year members meet together at 40 Brunswick Square under the watchful eye of the Hogarth portrait of their great benefactor Captain Thomas Coram: in June at Coram Day, hosted by the governors and staff of Coram Family; in October on Charter Day to remember the signing of the Charter that established the Foundling Hospital by George II in 1739; and in December for a Christmas carol service. During their childhood these former pupils were indeed each other's only family. Some were foster brothers and sisters. What brought them together is, as often as not, the difficult times they shared and the sense of guilt and rejection and being 'different' that many have carried throughout their lives as they have tried to find out who they are and where they came from. But there is fun and laughter too, and many good friendships that have lasted over the years.

Drawing on contemporary sources and first-hand accounts from the archives,[1] as well as interviews with former pupils and staff, this book tells the story of one of the most remarkable institutions in England, the first children's charity, established in 1739 – the Foundling Hospital. During its long life as a residential institution, the Hospital provided a home for 25,000 children for their entire childhood. The story is told against a background of changing social mores: starting in the golden age of philanthropy; moving on through the Victorian era with its distinction between the deserving and undeserving poor and the need to 'rescue' children, particularly illegitimate children, from their fickle parents; and finally into the era of the post-war welfare state when the influences of child psychiatry and psychology drew attention to the importance of children's emotional well-being, and of supporting parents wherever possible so that their children could stay with them.

The book begins with a short biography of Captain Thomas Coram, a man of extraordinary energy and tenacity who was dismayed at the sight of children dying on the dung heaps of London. After seventeen years of campaigning, he managed to persuade sufficient 'persons of quality and distinction' to support his petition to the King to grant a Royal Charter for what he called his 'darling project' – the building of the Foundling Hospital in a green field site in Bloomsbury.

The next two chapters recount the detailed work required of the Court of Governors as, with meticulous care, they put in place systems for receiving babies into the institution; for christening them with new names; for placing them with wet-nurses or foster parents in the country for five years; and then for bringing the children back into the Hospital. Once there, they were provided with excellent health care and education fit for their station in life, but with little knowledge of their emotional needs, before the boys were apprenticed to learn a trade and the girls to domestic service. Even at this stage, particularly during the years of open admissions, the governors were struggling to make ends meet as the demands were always greater than their ability to meet them. The daily routines are described – routines that appear to have changed little until the Second World War. We hear about what the children did, what they ate, what they wore, what they were taught in school, what happened when they were sick, and – the highlight for many – the music in the chapel.

Chapter IV explores the relationship between the Foundling Hospital and two of the artistic giants of the eighteenth century – the artist William Hogarth and the composer George Frideric Handel, both of whom helped to raise substantial sums of money for the charity and both of whom became governors. Hogarth was also an inspector of wet-nurses. Their legacy lives on in the extraordinary collection of paintings, other artefacts and musical scores that are now on display in the Foundling Museum.

Chapter V explores the very limited changes that were introduced into the Foundling Hospital during the nineteenth century, mainly changes in admission criteria which stipulated that the child must be illegitimate and the mother unsupported, but able to make her way in life if the child was accepted into the Hospital. Key figures of this period were Charles Dickens, who lived very close to the Foundling Hospital and wrote of his visits, and through whose pen pictures we get such a vivid sense of lives of the poor children of London; and his friend John Brownlow, a foundling who grew up in the Hospital and went on to serve it for fifty-eight years, only retiring from his post as secretary through ill health.

The next two chapters take us through the first half of the twentieth century. After a century of limited change, the governors found themselves having to sell the Foundling Hospital site, move the children to Redhill on a temporary basis, purchase the site and build the new school at Berkhamsted, then move the children to Berkhamsted. Finally, after a comparatively short space of time and under pressure from the government and the

1948 Children Act, they reduced the numbers of children living permanently in what was now called the Thomas Coram Schools, and returned them to their foster parents. The buildings were sold to Hertfordshire County Council in 1950 and by 1955 the now renamed Thomas Coram Foundation for Children returned to its base in London and became a fostering agency.

Chapter VII draws on interviews and written accounts by former pupils, recollected with varying emotions, many years after they had left school. There were undoubtedly some harsh and difficult times, as there are in many boarding schools, the difference being that most children attending boarding school know that they will be going home for the holidays. What was most painful for these men and women was the attitude towards them as illegitimate children, and the sense of guilt, inferiority and rejection that this implied. In contrast to the regime within the school, the memories of the first five years in the country with foster parents, and the month spent under canvas in the summer, are mainly full of sunshine, laughter and freedom.

Chapter VIII brings the Coram story up to date. From 1955 to 2005 Coram Family (as it is now called) has responded to the changing needs of children and families whilst continuing with the innovative tradition of its founder. At the same time it has moved away from residential care towards a focus on finding substitute families (through adoption) for children who cannot live with their birth families. Coram Family has also developed a range of community based services for vulnerable children and families that promote resilience and help children to develop the capacity to thrive in often difficult circumstances. Although very few children are now abandoned, and the dung heaps in the streets have disappeared, there are still too many children who do not get the love and care that they deserve and whose lives are blighted through the lack of a supportive family.

The chapter also relates the tale of the establishment of the Foundling Museum, set up as a separate charity to display the historical treasures and to bring alive the legacy of Thomas Coram and the story of London's forgotten children.

Chapter IX concludes with reflections on this legacy, pulling out some key themes from the 265-year history of this unique organisation: the changing view of childhood; social perceptions of illegitimacy; and the particular contribution that the Foundling Hospital made to the history of childcare as well as its role as the first modern charity. There were times when the organisation led the way in developing new thinking about the care of children who were not able to live with their own families, and others when it took longer than it should to respond to the need for change. Today Coram Family continues to take risks on behalf of children and again lives up the pioneering spirit of its founder.

A final chapter in this revised edition, written in 2022, explores more recent research into the Foundling Hospital archives, and brings the work of the charity Coram, and the Foundling Museum, up to date.

Thomas Coram: The Man and his Mission

The man who gave his name to the first and only Foundling Hospital in England was a remarkable individual. He was determined and compassionate, sometimes brusque, and a man 'of obstinate, persevering temper, as never to desist from his first enterprise, whatever obstacles lie in his way.'[1] His perseverance was needed. Coram was seventy-one by the time the Hospital received the Royal Charter, and he had spent much of the previous seventeen years on what he called his 'darling project'.

Coram's biographer summarises his key qualities:

He was a man of startling integrity in an age of corruption, a man prepared to use his own limited resources to gain his objects, with little expectation of personal reward apart from the satisfaction of having contributed to the public good. From a modest family background, without wealth or a patron, in an age when both were considered a necessity, he triumphed through his own energy, persistence, and enterprise, combined with a rough charm of manner, made the more appealing on account of his patent honesty. Unfortunately his fierce temper, together with his injudicious habit of responding in an intemperate manner, both verbally and in writing, to perceived or real injustices, made for difficulties throughout his life.[2]

Thomas Coram was born in Lyme Regis in 1668, the son of John and Spes Coram. His mother died when Thomas was three, shortly after giving birth to his brother William, who also died. His father was left to bring up Thomas on his own, and perhaps the fact that Thomas makes almost no mention of his father in letters suggests that this was a difficult time and relationships were strained. Coram describes his comparative lack of education and impoverished early years in a letter written in 1724:

> For my part I am no Judge in Learning I understand no Lattin nor English nither, well, for though Through Mercy I discended from virtuous good Parentage on both sides as any Body, they were Famelies of Strict hon'r and honesty and always of Good Reputation amongst the better sort of people, Yet I had no Learning, my Mother Dying when I was Young, My Father Marryed again 4 or 5 years after at Hackney Near this City. I went to sea, out of my Native place, the Little Town of Lyme in the West of England at 11 years and a half old until 5 years after my Father sent for me hither and put me apprentice to a Shipright.[3]

We have no written record of Thomas Coram's early life at sea but as such a young apprentice, life is likely to have been hard. Aged sixteen, his father apprenticed him to a shipwright, a good foundation for a future career for a young man in a country with a merchant fleet that was expanding in line with its overseas trade and colonies. His apprenticeship was followed by two years working in shipyards in London before he left for New England aged only twenty-five but with a considerable amount of relevant experience.

Although he is best known for his work with the Foundling Hospital right at the end of his life, New England and the new colonies were to be a focus for much of the middle years of Coram's life. The ten years that he spent in New England in particular had far reaching effects, both positive and negative. Shipbuilding was already well established when Thomas Coram arrived in Boston in 1693 but when he moved to Taunton (on a river south of Boston) in 1697 it was to set up the first ship builders.

He got off to a good start: buying land, building himself a house, establishing a business and – in 1700 – marrying Eunice Wayte from one of Boston's oldest families. He became involved in the Christian education of the Indians, though despite his lifelong commitment to fighting for the underdeveloped, he was never directly involved in the abolition of the slave trade. He was energetic and hard-working and his business went well, but it was not long before he fell out with the local people. He was seen as an arrogant outsider, and his contempt for the local people included his dislike of their Free Church religion which did not sit well with his Anglicanism. His ships were attacked and burnt, and he narrowly escaped being murdered. Court cases were brought and eventually, burdened by debt, he returned to England. Typically, his final gesture was to bequeath a sum of money to the people of Taunton to enable them to build an Anglican church. Resplendent with reproductions of Hogarth's portrait of Coram and a stained-glass window in Coram's memory, St Thomas' church (which still stands today), is Coram's most lasting memorial in America.

Back in London, Coram was determined to return to America. He became involved in plans for the settlement of Maine and Nova Scotia. Writing to his brother the Prime Minister, Horatio Walpole described him as 'the honestest and most disinterested and the most knowing person about the plantations that I have ever talked with'. Coram put much unpaid time and effort into petitions arguing for land to be put aside in the province of Georgia for disbanded soldiers and settlers from England. He was appointed as trustee for the settlement of Georgia by George II, the highest public office that he attained. He became involved in further trading and petitioning in relation to Hamburg, developing and using his extensive networks of contacts. The failure of the South Sea Company in 1720, which left thousands of people with considerable losses, led to a more cautious approach to investment and Coram had to put his plans for settlements in America on temporary hold.

The London that Coram returned to was a whirl of contrasting sounds, sights and smells. The social historian Roy Porter asks whether Georgian London had become a monster or a miracle. On the one hand there was its wealth, its energy and its diversity, illustrated by Johnson's famous claim that 'When a man is tired of London, he is tired of life'. On the other, Porter cites the moralists who lacerated London: 'Henry Fielding exposed its vanity, deceits and cheats and William Hogarth's capital was all disease and violence, filth, noise, falling building and fallen women, chaos, poverty, drunkenness, suicide, distress, disarray, infidelity and insanity'.[4] All of these are vividly illustrated in Hogarth's paintings and etchings, not least in the well-known *Gin Lane*: the gin craze had reached a point by the 1740s where two pints a week were being drunk by every man, woman and child in London.

Many of the streets were open sewers, drinking water was contaminated and the atmosphere was thick with sulphurous coal smoke. Huge numbers of children survived on the streets by prostitution, begging, boot blacking, mudlarking (scavenging on the Thames mud) and pickpocketing – as personified a century later by the 'Artful Dodger' in Dickens' *Oliver Twist*.

As growing urbanisation began to replace a largely agricultural way of life and patterns of agricultural communities were destroyed, there was a rise in homelessness and in illegitimacy. In London there was alarm at the increase in poverty – which tended to be seen as a moral defect – and the threat that it posed to social order. The Poor Law system that had been established in 1572 (and was to remain in place until 1834) was struggling to cope with the demands made on it. The problems of the poor had far outstripped the ability of the parish relief system to cope, and there was a feeling that the parish system encouraged idleness, which led to vice and crime. A distinction was made between the deserving and the undeserving poor, and there was a strong view that the poor should work. Defoe, for example, said that true poverty was not among beggars but among families where death or sickness deprived them of the labour of the father.[5] In this climate, unmarried mothers and their illegitimate children were seen as a particular burden, combining moral failing and a lack of financial responsibility.[6]

The mortality rate for children at the beginning of the century was extremely high – one in three babies died before the age of two, and one in two of those who survived died before the age of fifteen. In the workhouses the death rate was over 90% and in one Westminster parish only one in 500 foundlings survived. For lone mothers, both the mother and her child were at risk. If a mother gave birth alone and her baby died, she would be suspected of having killed the baby and would have been arrested. The Old Bailey Sessions' papers are full of such cases, and mothers who were found guilty were executed.[7] Around ten to fifteen women were tried for child murder every year in England throughout the eighteenth century and although many were acquitted, those who were found guilty would have been either transported or hanged. Even those who were acquitted would have found their lives in ruins, with few prospects of employment or marriage. Unsurprisingly, this led to an alarming increase in the number of abandoned babies left in churches or hospitals or the new workhouse in

Bishopsgate. Many mothers would have seen abandonment as a temporary expedient until their fortunes improved, and huge efforts were made to find the mothers of such foundlings so that they would not be a burden on the parish.

When Coram decided to give up his seafaring life he found himself with more time on his hands and he began to notice the appalling state of London's streets, with their heaps of rubbish, dead cats and dogs and abandoned babies. While he continued to work on his plans for settlements in Maine, Georgia and Nova Scotia over the next twenty or so years, the germ of a new project was born, which was perhaps given greater force by the inability of his wife to have children, and the early loss of his young brother William. Addison had first highlighted the plight of foundlings in *The Guardian* in 1713:

> I shall mention a Piece of Charity which has not yet been exerted among us, and which deserves our attention the more, because it is practised by most of the Nations about us. I mean a Provision for Foundlings, or for those Children who for want of such a Provision are exposed to the Barbarity of cruel and unnatural parents. One does not know how to speak of such a subject without horror: but what multitudes of infants have been made away with by those who brought them into the world and were afterwards ashamed or unable to provide for them! There is scarce an assize where some unhappy wretch is not executed for the murder of a child … It is certain that which generally betrays these profligate women … is the fear of shame,

or their inability to support those whom they give life to … This is a subject that deserves our most serious consideration.[8]

It was the burden of shame that Coram particularly emphasised. He also thought that despair, amounting almost to insanity, was a main cause of infanticide, as is clear from John Brownlow's account of the Foundling Hospital written in 1847:

> He found that it [infanticide] arose out of a morbid morality then possessing the public mind, by which an unhappy female, who fell a victim to the seductions and false promises of designing men, was left to hopeless contumely and irretrievable disgrace. Neither she nor the offspring of her guilt appear to have been admitted within the pale of human compassion; her false step was her final doom, without even the chance, however desirous, of returning to the road of rectitude.[9]

According to the philanthropist and author Jonas Hanway, attempts to set up such a hospital earlier in Queen Anne's reign had not been supported by merchants because of the prejudice of public opinion – 'ill grounded prejudices that such an undertaking might seem to encourage persons in vice, by making it too easy provision for their illegitimate children'.[10] The opposition case was that parish officers would escape their duties and the poorer classes would shelve their responsibilities, as can be seen from a response to Hanway's support for Coram: 'In a

Protestant Country like Britain, where the Poor are so amply provided for' it would reflect:

> dishonour, not only upon the State, but upon the whole community, as it tacitly implies either a Want of Wholesome Laws, or a Want in the due execution of them. A Foundling ... reflects the highest disgrace on Human Nature, and supposes a depravity in the Morals, and a degeneracy in the Affections of Rational Beings ... Destructive of all Social Order and Concord.[11]

Over the next seventeen years Coram saw at first hand the double standards that were in play, where illegitimate births amongst the aristocracy were seen as unfortunate but acceptable, whilst the provision of any support for the poor working classes was seen as encouraging promiscuous sex. A combination of this hypocrisy and the disaster of the South Sea bubble bursting (which made many potential backers suspicious of joint stock companies), were going to present Coram with many obstacles.

The response that Coram received for his plans to establish a Foundling Hospital were in stark contrast to the City's willingness to establish Christ's Hospital in 1552 for the poor children of the local parishes, although by 1676 this institution was prohibiting the admission of illegitimate children, taking only children born in wedlock. The 1722 Poor Relief Act gave church wardens and overseers of the poor the right to establish workhouses to accommodate children and adults, but conditions were poor, infant mortality rates very high, and any concept of education for the children had been superseded by the notion that they should be put to work as soon as possible. As a committed Anglican, Coram was disgusted at the Church's hostility to his proposals for destitute children, though he did find support from the Dean of St Patrick's Cathedral in Dublin, Jonathan Swift. Writing in 1720 in his satirical pamphlet *A modest Proposal for preventing the Children of Poor People from being a Burthen toe their Parents or Country and for making them beneficial to the Publick*, Swift tried to shock the public into action by proposing that pauper children be fattened and reared at public expense for gentlemen of refined taste: 'A child will make two dishes as an entertainment for friend, and when the family dines alone, the fore or hind quarter will make a reasonable dish, seasoned with a little pepper or salt will be very good boiled on the fourth day'.

Although the Church did not support his plans, it is important to see Coram's endeavours in the context of the eighteenth-century view of the role of the State. As Porter points out, no one dreamed that it was the government's responsibility to educate children, heal the sick, house the homeless, provide pensions for the elderly or rehabilitate offenders:

> This is not to imply that our Georgian forebears were so heartless as to believe that the weak should go to the wall: they weren't. But the government, all agreed, was mainly there to fight the French and uphold law and order. Social problems should be dealt with on a

personal and parish basis, and many important matters
were best left to charity.[12]

And it was indeed a time of energetic philanthropy,
with five new hospitals established within a space of a
few years – including Westminster, Guys, St Georges and
Middlesex – and dozens of charity schools and other
philanthropic enterprises.

The lack of support from the Church within this
overall context of philanthropy led Coram to a stroke
of genius. If the merchants, the Churchmen and the
noblemen would not support him, he would approach
the ladies of the aristocracy, who he referred to as ladies
of 'quality and distinction'. He was helped in this by
his friend the Revd Thomas Bray, vicar of St Botolph
without Aldgate who, through his work in establishing the Society for the Propagating of the Gospel, had
supported Coram's work in relation to the American
colonies. Bray discovered that the organisation of
L'Hopital pour les Enfants Trouvés in Paris was run and
supported by women, and wrote a pamphlet proposing
a similar Hospital should be set up in London. He took
both a religious and a secular/utilitarian approach. He
urged the Christian duty of saving the lives of innocent
children, but also pointed out that the children saved
would, with proper training, lower parish rates and be
useful in service as apprentices instead of begging and
stealing. Spurred on by the success of the pamphlet, and
with the help of Newman, secretary to the SPCK[13] and
formerly in service with the Duke of Somerset, Coram
began to plan how to gain access to the titled ladies that

he would need to sign his petition. The petition itself is in Coram's inimitable forthright style:

> Whereas among the many excellent designs and insti-
> tutions of charity, which this nation and especially the
> city of London has hitherto encouraged and estab-
> lished, no expedient has yet been found out for the
> preventing the frequent murders of poor miserable
> infants at their birth; or for suppressing the inhuman
> custom of exposing new born infants to perish in
> the street; or putting out such unhappy foundlings to
> wicked and barbarous nurses, who undertake to bring
> them up for a small and trifling sum of money, too
> often suffer them to starve for the want of due suste-
> nance or care; or if permitted to live, either turn them
> into the streets to beg or steal, or hire them out to
> loose persons ... For a beginning to redress so deplor-
> able a grievance, and to prevent as well the effusion of
> so much innocent blood ... and to enable them, by an
> early and effectual care of their education to become
> useful members of the commonwealth, we whose
> names are underwritten, being deeply touched with
> compassion for the sufferings and lamentable condi-
> tion of such poor abandoned helpless infants, ... and
> for the better producing good and faithful servants
> from amongst the poor and miserable cast off children
> or foundlings ... are desirous to encourage and willing
> to contribute towards erecting an hospital for infants.[14]

Two highly publicised cases of illegitimacy amongst aristocratic families helped to heighten awareness of the different views taken within different social classes, and with the first signature from the Duchess of Somerset, Coram was on his way. He took advantage of the relatively close-knit circle of aristocratic women, many of whom had first-hand experience of illegitimacy within their families, and by 1730 had the signatures of sixteen ladies of high rank, with a further five signing four years later. The Ladies Petition was presented to King George II in 1735.

Partly thanks to the support of their wives, Coram was now beginning to build up lists of supporters from the aristocracy and courtiers. By 1737 he had enlisted the support of twenty-five dukes, thirty-one earls, twenty-six other members of the peerage and thirty-eight knights. His powers of persuasion had also gained the support of the entire Privy Council headed by the Prince of Wales, together with the Prime Minister Robert Walpole and the speaker of the House of Commons Arthur Onslow MP. This was no mean feat for a man of such humble origins, and was a tribute to his tenacity and per-suasive powers, as well as the leather of his boots, as he walked many miles each day to follow up leads to add to his list. The final petition included an amazing 375 signa-tures, with his own name at the end of the list. [15]

Later in 1735 Coram gathered signatures of Justices of the Peace, and these three petitions were submitted to the King in Council on 21 July 1737. The King referred them to a committee of the Privy Council, which in turn asked the Attorney General and Solicitor General for their opinions. The final lists, together with the names of the first governors to whom the charter would be granted, were confirmed by the King in Council on 22 March, and included some 172 of the 375 men named as governors, with the Duke of Bedford as the first president. In selecting governors Coram chose men of wealth and of influence, but also merchants who were probably known to him personally. The 172 men who agreed to become governors were aged between twenty-one and eighty, and Coram called on them all individually, walking many miles each day. He had no models to work to in setting up this first charity, but his emphasis on wealth and influence would not be far from the make-up of some charitable boards today. It is striking that no clergy were included apart from the archbishops of Canterbury and York and the bishop of London, and there were no women – the first woman governor was not appointed until the 1940s.

The charter establishing the Hospital for the Maintenance and Education of Exposed and Deserted Young Children was signed by King George II on 14 August 1739 and the Great Seal was affixed to it on 17 October. The seal was designed by Coram, and based on the biblical story of Pharoah's daughter finding the foundling Moses in the bulrushes – a theme that Hogarth was to take up in one of his paintings for the Hospital.

The first meeting of the governors took place in Somerset House, where Coram, now aged seventy, read out the words of the charter in front of the 170 assembled governors, and then made a moving speech to the new president of the Foundling Hospital:

My Lord, Duke of Bedford,
    It is with inexpressible pleasure I now present your grace, at the head of this noble and honourable

corporation, with his Majesty's royal charter, for establishing an Hospital for exposed children, free of all
expense, through the assistance of some compassionate great ladies and other good persons.

I can, my lord, sincerely aver, that nothing would
have induced me to embark in a design so full of difficulties and discouragements, but a zeal for the service
of his Majesty, in preserving the lives of great numbers
of his innocent subjects.

The long and melancholy experience of this nation
has too demonstrably shewn, with what barbarity
tender infants have been exposed and destroyed for
want of proper means of preventing the disgrace, and
succouring the necessities of their parents.

The charter will disclose the extensive nature and
end of this Charity, in much stronger terms than I can
possibly pretend to describe them, so that I have only
to thank your Grace and many other noble person-
ages, for all that favourable protection which hath
given life and spirit to my endeavours.

My Lord, although my declining years will not
permit me to hope seeing the full accomplishment
of my wishes, yet I can now rest satisfied, and is what
I esteem an ample reward of more than seventeen
years' expensive labour and steady application, that I
see your Grace at the head of this charitable trust,
assisted by so many noble and honourable gentlemen.

Under such powerful influences and directions, I
am confident of the first success of my endeavours, and
that the public will one day reap the happy and lasting
fruits of your Grace's and this Corporation's measure,

and as long as my life and poor abilities endure, I shall
not abate of my zealous wishes, and most active services for the good prosperity of this truly noble and
honourable Corporation.[16]

It is interesting to reflect on why Coram finally
succeeded in setting up the Hospital in 1739 when
he had met with such resistance twenty years earlier.
There are a number of probable reasons: it was now
nineteen years since the South Sea bubble fiasco and
some confidence in financial investment had returned.
There had been a marked increase in concern regarding
illegitimacy and subsequent infanticide. There was need
for an increase in the population to support the wars
against the French and perhaps for the first time ever
children were seen as a national resource. There was, as
we have seen, a growing commitment to philanthropy
not just amongst the aristocracy but also amongst the
newly-rich merchant and professional classes. And there
was the crucial importance of the Ladies Petition, and
of the support of Queen Caroline who had been very
supportive before her death in 1737. Coram realised
the potency of the power of example, and realised that
benevolence would be seen as a means of furthering the
social positions of Hospital supporters.

His achievement as an innovator was remarkable. The
Foundling Hospital set the pattern of charitable organisations in England, many of them surviving to this day. He
modelled the Board on a joint stock company and, unlike
counterparts in continental Europe, remained independ-
ent from the Church. He found ways of engaging 'the

great and the good', and in particular their wives – in today's parlance the 'ladies who lunch' – from both the aristocracy and the merchant classes. And he relentlessly kept his sights on his grand plan.

Coram, essentially a man who preferred to work on his own, now found himself part of a powerful team. Four days after the signing of the charter some thirty-one governors, including Coram, were elected to a General Committee which approved the seal and set about planning for the opening of the Hospital. The Duke of Montagu offered the use of his house in Great Russell Street but Coram thought this unsuitable and followed up a plan of his own. Montagu House went on to become the base for the British Museum. There were other challenges to contend with, not least the need to amend the charter through an Act of Parliament, which did not receive royal assent until April 1740.

Hogarth had been one of those present at the meeting in Somerset House and had designed a headpiece for the official fundraising letter (see illustration 1). He now proposed to paint Coram's portrait. He admired Coram's honest and straightforward approach to caring for destitute children, and like Coram he had had a difficult and poor childhood, and had no children of his own. Hogarth also had his own career to think about, and was keen to impress on society that he was as skilful a painter as any foreign trained artist from France or Italy.[17]

During 1740 and 1741 the General Committee met twice a week and Coram did not miss a meeting. Subscriptions and legacies continued to come in, and the governors began to research how other Foundling

Hospitals in Europe – such as those in Venice, Florence, Paris, Turin and Holland – operated. They came to the view – very enlightened in view of what we now know about the importance of close and consistent relationships during the first years of life – that the children should be wet-nursed in the country during their first three years, and they began to seek out healthy nurses. Baby clothes were ordered, and staff were appointed. The search for a building continued and a house in Hatton Garden was leased for six years as a temporary base whilst the Hospital was being built. On the first anniversary of the signing of the charter – 17 October 1740 – an agreement was reached with Lord Salisbury for the purchase of fifty-six acres of land in Ormond Street, between Lamb's Conduit Street and Southampton Row.

The first announcement that the Hospital was ready to receive children was made in March 1741. It read as follows:

On Wednesday 25th of this instant March at eight at night and from that time until the house is full, their house over against the charity school in Hatton Garden will be open for children under the following regulations; that no child exceed in age two months nor shall have the French Pox or disease of like nature; all children to be inspected and the person who brings it to come in at the outer door and not to go away until the child is returned or notice given of its reception. No question asked whatsoever of any person who brings a child, nor shall any servant of the Hospital presume to enquire on pain of being dismissed ...

The narrow circumstances of the Hospital confin-
ing governors to a limited number, that everyone
may know when such numbers shall be completed, a
notice will be posted that the house is full. If any particular marks are left with the child great care will be
taken for their preservation. Each child will be baptised Church of England by a minister of the Church
unless such child has already been baptised.[18]

When the children were admitted, a detailed description of each child was made and any notes or token were
immediately sealed by the steward to protect the identity
of the mother. The children were all baptised, whether
they had been previously baptised or not, and were given
names chosen by the governors – the first boy was baptised Thomas Coram and the first girl Eunice Coram.
    Preparations were made for 25 March. Concerns in the
parish of St Andrew that children who were rejected might
be left by their mothers and become a charge on the parish
led to the involvement of two watchmen and two con-
stables. Inside the house ten governors, including Thomas
Coram, awaited the arrival of the first children. The minutes from the Daily Committee describe in vivid detail
what happened:

The Committee met at 7 o'clock in the Evening.
They found a great number of People crowding
about the door, many with Children and others for
Curiosity. The Committee were informed that several Persons had offer'd children, but had been refused
admittance. The Order of the Gen'l Committee being

that the House sho'd not be opened till Eight o'clock
at Night. And this Committee was resolved to give
no Preference to any person whatever ... At Eight
o'clock the Lights in the Entry were Extinguished,
the outward Door was opened by the Porter, who was
forced to attend at that Door all night to keep out
the Crowd. Immediately the Bell rung and a woman
brought in a Child. The Messenger let her into the
Room on the Right hand, and carried the child
into the Steward's Room, where the proper Officers
together with Dr Nesbitt and some other Govrs. were
constantly attending to inspect the Child according to the Directions of the Plan. The child being
inspected was received, Numbered and the Billet of
its Discription enter'd by three different Persons for
greater Certainty. The Woman who brought the Child
was dismissed without being seen by any of the Govrs.
or asked any questions whatsoever. Immediately
another child was brought and so continually until
30 children were admitted 18 of whom were Boys and
12 Girls being the number the House is capable of
containing. Two children were refused, one being too
old and the other appearing to have the Itch.

About twelve o'Clock, the House being full the
Porter was Order'd to give Notice of it to the Crowd
who were without, who thereupon being a little
troublesome One of the Govrs went out, and told
them that as many Children were already taken in
as Cou'd be made Room for in the House and that
Notice shou'd be given by Publick Advertisement
as soon as any more Could possibly be admitted.

And the Govrs observing seven or eight women with Children at the Door and more amongst the Crowed desired them that they wou'd not Drop any of their Children in the Streets where they most probably must Perish but take care of them till they could have an opportunity of putting them into the Hospital which was hoped would be very soon and that every Body would immediately leave the Hospital without making any Disturbance which was immediately complied with great Decency, so that in two minutes there was not a Person to be seen in the Street except the Watch. On this Occasion the Expressions of Grief of the Women whose Children could not be admitted were Scarecely more observable than those of some of the Women who parted with their Children, so that a more moving Scene can't well be imagined.

All the Children who were received (except three) were dressed very clean from whence and other Circumstances they appeared not to have been under the care of the Parish officers, nevertheless many of them appeared as if Stupified with Opiate, and some of them almost starved, or as in the agones of Death thro' want of Food, too weak to Suck, or to receive Nourishment, and notwithstanding the greatest care appeared to be dying when the Govrs left the Hospital which was not till they had given prper Orders and seen all necessary Care taken of the children.[19]

It must have been a very moving experience for the onlookers and heartbreaking for the mothers, whether they had left their children or found that there was no room for them.

Mindful of the need to raise further donations, the governors encouraged visitors to the Hospital. The minutes continue:

> The next day many Charitable Persons of Fassion visited the Hospital, and whatever Share Curiosity might have in inducing any of them to come, none went away without shewing the most Sensible Marks of Compassion for the helpless Objects of this Charity and few (if any) without contributing something for their Relief.

The first baptism service attracted a large number of 'persons of quality and distinction' including the Duke of Bedford, the Duke and Duchess of Richmond and the Hogarths, almost all of whom had children named after them. Several babies died within days of admission, including the first babies named after Thomas and Eunice Coram, and out of the first thirty children, twenty-three died within the first few months. But many lived to be apprenticed. Many in those early days were named after distinguished public figures, although this practice was later dropped as the children began to claim to be related to their namesakes as they grew up.

Many of the children arrived with little fragments of material, written notes and other tokens. As Gillian Wagner points out in her biography of Coram, by no stretch of the imagination could child no. 53, admitted on 17 April be classified as deserted or exposed:

The paper pinned to the child was carefully written by an educated hand. It read 'This is to certify that this infant has been baptised by a minister of the Church of England and named George – whose surname is Hanover, begs if asked for by that name that he may be seen if agreeable to the Rules of the Hospital'.[20]

The child was described as male, 'about ten days old and dressed in white satin sleeves bound up with blue mantua, a fine double cambric cap with double cambric border, and three fine diaper clouts. Extremely clean and neat'.[21] We do not know if the governors were aware of the details of George Hanover, or if, as was the custom, the mother's anonymity was preserved and the details sealed up immediately.

Having lived to see the realisation of his dream, Thomas Coram's last years were less happy and fulfilling. His dear wife Eunice had died in 1740, and in 1742 he was not reappointed on to the General Committee. He was accused of spreading malicious rumours about the behaviour of two of the governors, and was thought to be the author of a letter pointing out a number of irregularities in how the hospital was run. The first chief nurse had been dismissed after a month, and her place had been taken by Sarah Wood, the laundry maid. There were rumours that Sarah Wood had miscarried in the grounds of the Hospital, and she was eventually charged with immodesty, dishonesty, drunkenness and dismissed. The governors' committee, against whom the allegations were made, did not attend meetings for ten months. But the crime that Coram committed was to speak his mind and talk publicly about a private matter and for this his fellow governors could not forgive him.

It could not have been easy for Coram to find himself sidelined by the institution to which he had given himself so wholeheartedly. The Foundling Hospital too suffered from the loss of its chief fundraiser, with a dramatic fall in subscriptions in the two years following his ejection from the Management Committee. With time on his hands, Coram began drafting a charter for another Foundling Hospital, but this came to nothing. Despite being the most fashionable charity in London, for the next 150 years the Foundling Hospital was the only charity in the country to care for illegitimate children.

In 1746, after an absence of four years, Coram began to visit the Foundling Hospital again and became a familiar sight, sitting in his red coat, in the arcade in the grounds of the Hospital handing out gingerbread men to the children with tears in his eyes. He also attended christenings in the chapel, as godfather to more than twenty foundlings. His personal circumstances were not good, and as he reached his eighties some of the governors began to realise how poor he was. A subscription was raised, to which the Prince of Wales made a substantial contribution, and Coram lived for his last two years in relative comfort. In 1749 he received the freedom of the borough from the mayor and corporation of Lyme. There are no records of who cared for him during his final months, but on 29 March 1751 the governors received notification that he had died.

Ignored during his later life, the governors planned a funeral befitting Coram's achievements. The funeral

service was held in the chapel, which was by now completed, with the choirs of Westminster Abbey and St Paul's
Cathedral. Six of the governors supported the pall and
the rest followed the coffin. The funeral was widely
reported, with *Read's Weekly Journal* reporting that the
galleries were filled with gentlemen and ladies all dressed
in mourning, and with great decency, and the order with
which the whole was conducted made it a 'very awful
sight.'[22] Coram was buried in the chapel vaults with an
inscription that recognised what he achieved:

Captain THOMAS CORAM
Whose Name will never want a Monument
So long as this Hospital shall subsist,
Was born in the year 1668.
A Man eminent in that most eminent Virtue,
the Love of Mankind
Little attentive to his Private Fortune,
And refusing many Opportunities of increasing it,
His Time and Thought were continually employed
In Endeavours to promote the Public Happiness,
Both in this Kingdom and elsewhere,
Particularly in the Colonies of North America
And his Endeavours were many Times crowned
With the desired success.
His unwearied Solicitation, for above Seventeen
Years together
Which would have baffled the Patience and Industry
Of any man less zealous in doing Good.
And his Application to Persons of Distinction
of both Sexes,

Obtained at length the Charter of Incorporation
Bearing the Date 17th October 1739,
FOR THE MAINTENANCE AND EDUCATION
OF EXPOSED AND DESERTED YOUNG
CHILDREN
By which many Thousands of Lives
May be preserved to the Public and employed in a frugal
And honest Course of Industry.
He died the 29th of March 1751, in the
84th Year of his Age,
Poor in Worldly Estate, rich in Good Works,
And was buried at his own Desire in the Vault under-
neath this Chapel (the first there deposited) at the
East End thereof, many of the Governors and other
Gentlemen attending the Funeral
to do Honour to his Memory.
READER
The Actions will show whether thou art sincere
In the Praises thou may'st bestow on him
And if thou has Virtue enough to commend his
Virtues,
Forget not to add also the Imitation of them.[23]

It is thought likely that Coram's friend Dr Brocklesby contributed to this epitaph. Brocklesby speaks of Coram's cheerfulness, frankness, warmth, affection and great simplicity of manners. 'What he thought, he spoke; what he wished, he declared without hesitation, pursued without relaxation or disguise, and never considered obstacles any further than to discover the means to surmount them.'[24] Brocklesby added that when Coram began to attempt to put his ideas for the Foundling Hospital into effect, he made the scheme the subject of his conversation 'that he might learn the sentiments of other men, and from thence form some notion whether what he had in view was practicable'. Coram found many supporters for his project, but it was no easy task. As Brocklesby says 'he found his expectations strongly disappointed by an infinity of cross accidents that would certainly have wearied out the patience of a man whose resolution had not been equal to the vehemence of his temper'.

During his long life Coram had exhibited the single minded determination that is the hallmark of innovators and pioneers. And he had learned patience, persistence and the art of petitioning – attributes required by all those who lead charitable organisations.

II

THE FOUNDLING HOSPITAL GETS UNDERWAY: THE FIRST SIXTY YEARS

While the first children were cared for in the temporary accommodation in Hatton Garden, building work on the Foundling Hospital began on the fifty-six acres purchased from Lord Salisbury. The site was at the northerly tip of London in an isolated area known as Lamb's Conduit Fields: its boundaries were Queen Square and Great Ormond Street to the south, Gray's Inn Road to the east, and Southampton Row and Woburn Place (then a field) to the west (see illustration 4). It was remote enough from the potentially evil influences of the big city to provide room for expansion, as well as fresh air for the children. One of the governors, Theodore Jacobson, drew up plans for the building, which was to be in plain brick, with two wings and a chapel built round a courtyard. The estimated cost was £6,500. Each wing would accommodate 192 children, two in a bed. Work started on the west wing in 1742 and the first children moved in on 1 October 1745.

The east wing was completed in 1748 and the chapel in 1753. The building was unostentatious and somewhat dull looking, apart from the chapel and the governors' rooms – particularly the Court Room and the picture gallery, which were to be used for fundraising purposes (see illustration 47).

When the governors had researched other foundling hospitals in Europe they concluded that their administration (largely within the Catholic Church) would not translate easily into the English context, and that the income at their disposal – around £600 a year – would not support an institution of comparable size. The Paris hospital, for example, cared for 3,150 children (who could be left anonymously in a revolving door), but the London governors felt that sixty children would be their upper limit in the immediate future.[1] This led to restrictions on admissions: infants had to be under two months old and free from venereal disease, scrofula, leprosy and other infectious diseases. They had to be brought to the hospital by their mother or some other person to allow the chief nurse and apothecary to examine them.

In other respects the Foundling Hospital followed the practice of other European hospitals. The babies were christened and then boarded out on arrival with nurses, usually wet-nurses, in the country until they were five, at which point they would be brought back to London. All of the institutions made some provision for the education and vocational training of their children, preparing the boys for an apprenticeship or sea service and the girls for domestic service. The Foundling governors proposed to teach their children reading but not writing, for they intended that the children:

> ... learn to undergo with Contentment the most
> Servile and laborious Offices; for notwithstanding the
> innocence of the Children, yet as they are exposed
> and abandoned by their Parents, they ought to submit
> to the lowest stations, and should not be educated in
> such a manner as may put them upon a level with
> the Children of Parents who have the Humanity
> and Virtue to preserve them, and the Industry to
> Support them.[2]

The children were to be educated to be useful, but not on an equal footing with more deserving legitimate children.

Great care was taken to record the identity of children placed in the wheel in European hospitals, and the London governors adopted equally detailed procedures for the children they admitted. A small leaden tag was attached to each child, bearing a number that referred to a sealed packet containing identifying records, including exact details of when the child was admitted, any distinguishing marks or features, and any clothes and other objects that were brought with the child. The details of every child admitted to the Hospital were kept in billets which are now bound into books.[3] For example the record might state that a child was 'well dressed', 'exceedingly neat', 'very finely dressed' or mention 'a fine cambrick cap with a laced border' or a 'pair of white brocaded silk shoes tied with a white riband'. One of the first children admitted in 1741 was 'a male child, about two months old, with white dimity sleeves, lined with white, and tied with red ribbon'. Many parents left tokens with their children whereby they could be identified should they be reclaimed. Some of these are on display today in the Foundling Museum – coins, buttons, ribbons, a bottle tag marked 'Ale', small pieces of jewellery, a hazelnut shell, and sometimes written notes and poems (see illustration 41). Many mothers expressed the hope that one day they would be reunited with their child – as in the note that came with Joseph, born on 28 April 1759:

> Hard is my Lot in deep Distress
> To have no help where Most should find
> Sure Nature meant her sacred laws
> Should men as strong as Women bind
> Regardless he, Unable I,
> To jeep this Image of my Heart
> Tis Vile to Murder! Hard to Starve
> And Death almost to me to part
> If Fortune should her favours give
> That I in Better plight may Live
> I'd try to have my Boy again
> And Train him up the best of Men.

Some notes leave us in little doubt as to the social status of the parents:

> Sirs,
>   This child is the son of a Gentleman and a Young Lady of fashion, you may assure yourselves that the

moment Circumstances will admit (which for the honour of both is and must be at present a secret) it will be taken way, and this Noble foundation be remitted all their expenses.

The governors gave detailed thought to the recruitment and management of staff, particularly in the first instance to the wet-nurses who were to care for the infants. All nurses were to be assessed for their suitability initially by the Committee but later by the local inspectors. They had to be free from infection and were required to keep the children neat and tidy and feed them appropriately once they were weaned from the breast. Any nurses daring to give a child strong liquors or opiates faced instant dismissal. Nurses were paid 2s a week in 1753, which was increased to 3s a week by 1796, but in addition:

> for the encouragement of Nurses to do their Duty, the Governors shall have power to give to every Nurse, who has had the care of any Child or Children for two years and upwards, a reward not exceeding Ten Shillings if the child shall appear to the Governors to be in a healthy and thriving condition.[4]

All wet-nurses or foster parents were under the care and inspection of their local inspector, one of a number of voluntary inspectors, usually the local squire, doctor or parson but often their wives or the wives of governors, including Jane Hogarth (wife of the artist William) who as an inspector had nineteen nurses under her supervision. The inspectors' role was central, pivotal to the success of the whole system, as without the presence of an inspector no child could be placed with a nurse.[5] They identified suitable wet-nurses in the areas where they lived and then supervised the nurses on behalf of the hospital once the babies were placed with them, carrying out all the administrative duties that this entailed. They reported regularly to the hospital on all aspects of this supervision, including the distribution and return of clothing supplied by the hospital and the provision of medicines and their use. They informed the authorities of illness, problems and deaths, arranged for transport and funerals, paid the wages and arranged for those children who survived to return to the hospital at the age of five. The inspectors were instrumental in setting standards of care and their communication with the nurses was central to the wellbeing of the children. And a considerable number of them were women, particularly upper class women – the wives of governors and their social circle. As Clark concludes in her account of inspectors in Berkshire:

> There was no precedent for the management and supervisory activities undertaken by women for the Foundling Hospital; neither had there been any previous recognition by a national organisation of women working for it on equal terms with men. This was perhaps the first time that women were recognised as being on equal terms as men for the work that they did.[6]

The inspectors brought huge commitment and administrative skills to their job for which, at this time, they were paid nothing. Some men and women were in post for fifteen or twenty years and dealing daily with difficult social and medical issues and managing a workforce of nurses as well as living their own lives. The Foundling Hospital could not have operated without them.

In the early days nurses came from Hayes in Middlesex, Kensington, Romford, Stoke Newington, Staines, Chalfont St Peter, Chertsey, Egham, Hampshire and Berkshire. Many became very attached to their charges and tried to keep them rather than return them to the Hospital when they reached the age of five or six, particularly during the period 1756–1760 when they stayed on for a year or more longer than usual.

Right from the start the governors were unable to meet the demand for admissions, and there were frequently more than 100 women with babies and only 20 places available. The women were admitted to the Court Room, which was strewn with sand for the occasion, and a system of balloting devised. The women drew a ball from a bag: those who drew a white ball were sent with their child for an examination; those with a black ball were rejected; and those with a red ball waited to see if any of the white ball babies were rejected following their examination (see illustration 5). But this system did nothing to increase the number of places and still only about a third of children brought to the hospital were admitted. About 100 children were admitted each year, and by December 1751 some 821 children had been admitted, of whom 228 had died in the country, 88 in the hospital and 4 had been claimed by relatives.

By 1752, when the new building was complete, the governors had 600 children on their books, although costs were considerably higher than the funds available to them. Their institution was the talk of the town. Owen describes the Foundling Hospital as 'the most imposing single monument erected by 18th century benevolence'[7] and the French writer Jean Andre Rouquet noted in 1755:

> They have lately built an hospital in London for exposed and deserted children, which this famous metropolis greatly wanted. We may say that in England everything is done by the people. This hospital is now a very large building and was raised by the subscriptions of a few private persons who were desirous of seeing such an establishment. The King subscribed to it like others, and the public benefactions are every day increasing.[8]

Unfortunately they were not increasing fast enough. The governors set up a committee to look at ways of raising additional funds and in February 1756 they approved a petition to the House of Commons asking for its support in extending the charity. The imminence of war with France, and a sense that England was suffering a decline in its population may well have led to a receptive view amongst members of parliament, for in April 1756 the House of Commons passed a resolution 'that enabling the Hospital for the maintenance of exposed and deserted young children to receive all the children which shall be offered is ye only method to render that charitable institution of lasting and general utility'. Parliament voted £10,000 to the Hospital on condition that all children offered between 1 June and 31 December 1756 should be received.

Thus began the 'general reception', the most challenging and often chaotic period of the Foundling Hospital's history. The governors appointed 140 more wet-nurses and advertised for children under two months old. Recent research shows that, unlike in some European hospitals, a basket was not hung at the gate for mothers to simply leave their baby in. On the first day 117 children were taken in, and 299 in the first week, some brought by their fathers against their mother's wishes. The governors struggled to keep their meticulous records, from which it is evident that many of this new influx of admissions came from the poorest parishes. But the records also show considerable numbers from St James Westminster and St George Hanover Square, parishes with large households employing many servants. The fine clothing and the valuable tokens left with some of these children suggest that whilst they may have been bastards they were also of high social status.

The governors struggled to appoint additional staff and to provide adequate supervision for the growing number of wet-nurses. During the first year of the general reception some 3,300 children were sent out to nurses as far away as Derbyshire and Yorkshire, as well as those in Surrey, Kent, Hertfordshire, Hampshire, Essex and Berkshire which were the counties used from 1794 onwards. The governors tried to protect the nurses against disease and exploitation and the vast majority of the thousands who took in foundling children appeared to have cared for them reasonably well. Governors themselves were encouraged to volunteer for inspection duties. There were occasional cases of unscrupulous inspectors exploiting nurses and failing to pay them. But most inspectors, responsible for supervising the nursing of many thousands of children, were meticulous in their duties, for which they received no remuneration.

The governors also set up a number of branch hospitals in areas where they felt that it would be relatively easy for them to find employment in agriculture and the textile industry for apprentices – Ackworth in Yorkshire in 1757 (now a secondary school run by the Society of Friends); Shrewsbury in 1758 (incorporated into Shrewsbury School in 1785); Aylesbury in 1759, Westerham in 1760 and Chester and Barnet in 1762. With just three clerical staff, the governors acquired properties, fitted them out, engaged staff and transported children all within a few months – an extraordinary feat. Ackworth was particularly successful as we can see from the voluminous correspondence of the Revd Lee, the rector of Ackworth and indefatigable governor and inspector of the Ackworth Hospital. It was also considered to be the healthiest of the Branch Hospitals, and received the worst medical cases and many disabled foundlings who would never be fit to become apprentices. His letters show him to have been an efficient and disinterested worker for the children, ingenious in his capacity for surmounting difficulty, well able to stand up for what he thought to be right against the directives of the London Hospital, guided by high ideals but contented to attend to detail.[9] He and

John Hargreaves the steward, got a caravan built to bring children from London, and over a fifteen-year period some 2,361 children were apprenticed from Ackworth, some of them going into the textile industries.

Not all of the branch hospitals were as lucky as Ackworth in their governors. For example, the group of men who came together to form a committee in Aylesbury, were led by the colourful local MP and High Sheriff of Buckinghamshire John Wilkes, described as 'the only famous citizen Aylesbury ever had.'[10] Wilkes was a man of action, a wit, a womaniser, a satirist and a sharp critic of the government. He was a governor of the Foundling Hospital and in this capacity offered to build and run a branch hospital in 1759. Wilkes himself was appointed treasurer to the Committee, which duly built a small hospital, taking about twenty children at a time. However from 1761 onwards it eventually became apparent that Wilkes was fiddling the books, drawing out money to pay the tradesmen but failing to do so. The governors eventually caught up with him (after he had fled to France having fought a duel) and in 1767 decided to close the Aylesbury Hospital which had caused them more financial and legal trouble than all the other branches, and threatened to tarnish their reputation.

During the four years of the general reception the governors bore the brunt of widespread abuse of the Poor Laws. Under the 1662 law of Settlement and Removal, a male bastard's legitimate descendants could be made a charge on the poor rate of the parish, so parish officers were keen to force men to marry their pregnant partners or else force the father to pay for the child's support. For parish officials eager to hold down the poor rates and harass the fathers of bastards, the opening of the Foundling Hospital was a godsend, and many children were sent to the hospital against the wishes of their mothers. The mortality rates in the Hospital during this period were 69% compared to 63% before open admissions,[11] and many babies died on their way to the hospital – as the novel *Coram Boy*[12] describes so vividly. A regular trade sprang up in bringing babies to the Foundling Hospital, as is evident from Brownlow's account of those days, written in 1847:

> a man on horseback, going to London with luggage in two panniers, was overtaken at Highgate, and being asked what he had in his panniers, answered 'I have two children in each; I have brought them from Yorkshire to the Foundling Hospital, and used to have eight guineas a trip; but lately another man has set up against me which has lowered my price'.[13]

The mortality rate of children nursed in the country also increased – no doubt due to the huge number of additional nurses required in a hurry as well as the ill health of the babies on arrival – and there were complaints from some parishes that too many children were being placed with them. The farmers of Hemsworth in Yorkshire, for example, combined to give their milk to the pigs rather than let the nurses have it, and the residents of Farnham in Surrey complained that the 200 foundlings being nursed there were leading to habits of idleness and drinking and were taking husbands away from industry and tempting them to live on their wives 'immoderate earnings'. For more recent research on this period, see Chapter X.

There were also rumblings in the press. An anonymous reviewer in the *London Chronicle* on 17 May 1757 – later identified as Dr Samuel Johnson – wrote that when:

> a few months ago I wandered through the Hospital, I found not a child that seemed to have heard of his Creed, or the Commandments. To breed up Children in this manner, is to rescue them from an early Grave, that they may find Employment for the Gibbet; from dying in Innocence, that they may perish by their Crimes.[14]

Critical pamphlets began to appear arguing against the separation of parents from their children. Joseph Massie, a writer on trade and finance, argued that parents would have no one to turn to in old age, and that children would not know how to parent their own children. He argued that the Hospital encouraged immorality and was excessively costly to the State. In response Joseph Hanway, a governor and strong supporter of the Hospital, argued that every life saved represented a net gain by the age of fifty of £176 10s. But the tide had begun to turn. Parliament began to reconsider its position as some MPs argued against support for the poor, who they saw as lazy, irresponsible and without moral standards. In March 1760 the government grant was terminated and the governors reclaimed their independence. The last child to be baptised under the open reception arrangements was called, with a nice touch of humour, Kitty Finis.

Parliament did not instantly withdraw all funding, but they did begin to introduce conditions for the grants, for example proposing that children should be apprenticed at age seven or earlier with a fee of £5 or £10. The governors resisted this proposal on the grounds that children were far too young at seven, and the fee would provide the wrong motivation for potential employers. The annual arguments continued, with governors making regular appearances before the public accounts committee, until parliament made a final grant in 1771 for the care of all children taken in up until 1760. By January 1770 the governors had apprenticed over 4,000 children. Although parliament saw their total grants of £546,000 as an expensive mistake, it was the first time that central government rather than the parish had seen itself as having some responsibility for abandoned children, using a charity as its agent. And as Hanway pointed out, the £102 for each child living to an age at which it could be apprenticed was in fact £265 in terms of value to the community.

Following the end of the period of general reception, the governors were unable to take many new children for some years. A few children went back to their parents, and it was agreed that boys could be apprenticed at an earlier age of eleven or twelve, but not the age of seven or eight that parliament had proposed. Some of the boys went to sea and some to agriculture and manufacturing, and most of the girls went into domestic service.

The governors took their responsibilities for the young apprentices seriously and checked on their progress until the boys reached the age of twenty-five and the girls twenty-one. The laws governing apprentices bound children by their indentures to husbandmen or tradesmen. The apprentices were obliged to stay in service until they were twenty-four, and the master was obliged to instruct them. Anyone practising a trade had to serve a seven-year apprenticeship. During the term of their apprenticeship the Foundling Hospital schoolmaster visited the boys, and the matron visited the girls. Any complaint from a foundling about their master was followed up and they would be removed if they were ill treated. Masters were required to ensure that children said their prayers and went to church regularly. Part of the agreement with their masters was that each apprentice should get £5 a year for their final three years. For the foundlings the apprenticeship offered a gateway to independence, ensuring a future that gave them a settlement and a trade, so that they would not be dependent on the parish.

The 1740 Act of Parliament enabled the governors to apprentice foundlings, and they put in place a system of vetting all potential masters. Children could only be placed with Protestants, and only under apprenticeship indentures. They were never placed in public houses, and were given instructions on how to behave when they left the Hospital.

Some foundlings were apprenticed to their foster fathers if they had a trade, for which a legal settlement was required as adoption was not authorised until 1926. Paul Holton, for example, child no. 15297, came into the Hospital in 1760 and went to a wet-nurse called Susan Holton in Wokingham. In 1766 he was apprenticed to the wine merchant in the town where he became very successful in business, becoming an alderman of the town.[15] There is a plaque to him in the local church, and performances of *Messiah* are still sung in aid of Coram in his memory. Relationships with foster families were often rather better than with their masters, and apprentices who ran away from their placements often returned to the families with whom they had spent their first five years.

Legacies had dwindled during the period of the parliamentary grant, and although the sale of the branch hospitals raised some income, few new children were taken in, with the exception of thirty-four children of military men who had been killed during the seven-year war with France. From 1756 until 1801 a few children were accepted on payment of £100, an arrangement that was almost certainly abused by high ranking women who could get rid of illegitimate babies with no questions asked.[16] However, most admissions were still from destitute unmarried women seduced by lovers with a promise of marriage and then deserted when they became pregnant.

From 1768 onwards admission was at the discretion of the General Committee and there were detailed inquiries about every child. A balloting system was reintroduced, and in order to reduce the crowds, mothers came without their babies on Wednesdays and those who drew a white ball returned with their child on a Saturday. The petitions of the mothers had to be corroborated, and the secretary or the steward would be sent to investigate whether the circumstances were as described in the petition. They were looking for assurances that the mother had a job to return to once her child had been admitted; that the pregnancy, if illegitimate, had occurred after a long-term relationship and that there had been a promise of marriage between the couple. There were still more applications than the governors could cope with, and the number of admissions depended on the funds available.

There was a decline in the rate of infant mortality in the Hospital when the general reception ended, and the infant mortality rate of 28.6% compared well with the rate in the Paris hospital of 80%. But the overall death rate rose steadily, and between 1760 and 1800 only 46% of the 2,000 children who were admitted during that period lived to be apprenticed. These figures, however, have to be seen in the context of 75% of poor children dying before the age of five. Apart from the period of open admissions, the death rate also was not as poor as that of foundling hospitals in Florence and elsewhere in Europe, largely due to the system of screening infants for ill health on arrival. The governors were also very efficient in their administrative systems, and three-quarters of infants were placed with nurses within a week of admission.[17]

The 2,000 children included an increasing number of parish children, following an act introduced by Joseph Hanway in 1767 which enabled the Foundling Hospital to take in illegitimate children, whilst the parishes would support their mothers. There was to be a monthly charge for this service, although some parishes refused to pay. The governors considered drafting an act to compel parishes to send pauper children to the Hospital and maintain them until they were ten, but nothing came of this, and the parishes gradually stopped sending the children.

There was also a discernible shift in the Foundling Hospital's purpose towards the end of the century. A statement from the treasurer in 1797 recognises a dual objective that Thomas Coram himself would undoubtedly have agreed with:

> The Foundling Hospital has Two Objects to preserve and educate Infants otherwise exposed to perish, and to restore the mothers to a course of Industry and Virtue so that almost every Act of the Charity is attended with a double Benefit, the preservation of the Child and of the Parent.[18]

By 1801 the governors had agreed that only illegitimate children were eligible for admission. The impact of this decision is considered in Chapter five.

A crucial part of the Foundling Hospital, for both religious and fundraising reasons, was the chapel (see illustration 6). It opened in 1753 after a series of fundraising concerts organised by Handel, whose involvement with the Foundling Hospital is described in Chapter four. Morning and evening preachers were appointed and charity sermons were preached, usually by a bishop. Music became an important part of the curriculum and a source of employment and income for some of the blind pupils. The services drew in large numbers of the great and good of the day, who paid to rent a pew on a regular basis and to attend concerts. Collections at services at the turn of the century were around £50 – a not inconsiderable sum at the time – and in 1802 the chapel earned £2,641 4s 7d.[19]

Before moving on to look at the experience of daily life in the Foundling Hospital, let us look briefly at the administrative and financial arrangements that were set up in this first sixty years. As was noted in the previous Chapter, some 375 governors were initially appointed, from a wide range of backgrounds, both from the nobility and the merchant and professional classes, and others were added at further meetings of the court. They were not required to be practising Christians, and there were few churchmen, and no women. Most of the work was done by the General Committee of some fifty governors, appointed annually which met on a weekly basis every Wednesday. As is decreed in the charter, in 1760 (and still indeed in 2006) the full court of governors met four times a year, plus an annual meeting. Not surprisingly, many of these governors did not attend, but much was expected of those on the General Committee. There was often continuity within families, with several generations of a family serving on the Court over 100 or more years. George Gregory MP, for example, was Treasurer or Chair of Governors for thirty-five years in the second half of the nineteenth century, and his son Roger, born in the Treasurer's house in the Hospital was – as Sir Roger Gregory – Treasurer from 1914 until his death in 1938. His daughter, who became Mrs Plant, was one of the first women to be made a governor.

In the early days there was no paid executive director and the senior official was called the Secretary. Executive decisions were taken by senior governors, particularly the Treasurer who lived in the Hospital, although he would have had other paid jobs. The Foundling Hospital was fortunate in the calibre and commitment of its treasurers and two in particular stand out from the early days – Taylor White, a judge, who held the reins for twenty-seven years from 1745 and oversaw the move into the new buildings and the beginning and end of the general reception; and Sir Charles Whitworth MP who took over from him and who, as a member of parliament, was responsible for ensuring that the parliamentary grant continued until all the children admitted during the open reception period were safely apprenticed. He also left £100 in his will in order to continue his gift of cakes for the children on New Year's Day.

The governors were somewhat paternalistic in their treatment of their employees, and stringent regulations were laid down in the by-laws for the appointment, conduct, and supervision of staff. A general provision relating to all officers, nurses and servants was that:

> they are to be persons of good character, and unencumbered with families of their own; they are to be persons professing the Protestant Religion … they are to avoid all contention with their fellow servants, and to behave with due respect to those placed over them … they are to promote the interests of the charity, and the health, industry and welfare of the children to the utmost of their power … they are not to game, or drink spirituous liquors … no servant or other person residing in the Hospital shall stay out later than nine o'clock in the winter, and ten o'clock in the summer without the leave of the Treasurer.[20]

The most senior employees were the Secretary who was responsible for the administration of the Hospital, and the Matron, who was not to exceed fifty years of age. The majority of employees were women and included wet- and dry-nurses, school mistresses, coat makers, cooks, kitchen servants, laundresses, housemaids and, during the general reception, a washer of the dead. The numbers varied, with sixty-six female employees during the general reception, and an average of thirty-three in the 1780s and 1790s. Most of the senior staff were men, including a steward, apothecary, clerk, secretary and a schoolmaster appointed in 1757. The men in more junior positions included a gardener, brewer, baker, porter and watch-man. The first foundling to be appointed to the staff is recorded in 1757 when John Grant became a clerk.

Financially the governors were dependent on public donations and legacies, apart from the period of the general reception when the grants from government brought their own difficulties. Having sidelined their most effective fund raiser – the founder Thomas Coram – early in the life of the Foundling Hospital, the governors struggled to meet the demand that their fledgling institution had created. Legacies accounted for just over a third of the income and one-off donations for another third, although public support fell off during the general reception period. Annual and special subscriptions, collections from the chapel services and income from investments and rents provided the rest. Among the fund raising schemes that proved successful – raising £200 a year – was the selling of the children's work: winding silk, making twine, knitting, spinning flax, and making shirts and weaving household linens. A more profitable line was the musical programmes in the chapel. And for a while ladies' breakfasts proved very popular with the fashionable women of London, so much so that in May 1749 the windows had to be boarded up to deter gate crashers. But there was never enough money to meet demand and, as McClure concludes, the Hospital's charitable revenues rose and fell on the tides of public interest and approval rather than in response to the economy.

As parliamentary support dwindled, the governors began to think of other ways of meeting the demands on them. As early as 1770 the Treasurer recommended that part of the Hospital's land should be let, but proposals to build houses met with opposition from local residents. However in the 1780s the governors' financial concerns led them to consider a more orderly development of the estate, in the hope that rental income would solve current difficulties. An anonymous pamphlet, probably written by one of the governors, attacked the scheme as causing deterioration in the healthy climate of the area, and proposing instead a reduction in the number of children cared for. Further in-fighting amongst the governors ensued, until the president, Lord North, was asked to convene a special meeting of the Court, which was attended by no less than ninety governors who supported the proposal. An agreement was reached with the Duke of Bedford to build on the land between the existing Hospital building and his private road (now Woburn Place) and the construction of Guilford, Bernard and Great Coram Streets was agreed, together with Tavistock Place and two new squares – Brunswick and Mecklenburgh. All of the leases required the governors' agreement before any shops or public houses could be opened. There were the usual legal problems, and concerns over poor workmanship and safety, and whether the rents could be collected adequately. But financially the development was a huge success and led to substantial increases in the Hospital's income. By the middle of the nineteenth century the annual ground rental equalled the original purchase price of the property.

The costs of running the Foundling Hospital were considerable. In 1788 it cost just over £7,000 to care for 192 children in the country and 317 in the Hospital in London with a total of 41 staff, a ratio of 8:1. The governors kept very close control of all expenditure, allowing the employees little authority to buy anything without their approval. They usually obtained competitive bids from suppliers and would often compare costs with officials of other institutions, particularly Christ's Hospital. As McClure concludes, reviewing the financial situation of the Hospital over the first sixty years, the governors raised the revenue with shrewdness and ingenuity and spent it with sound business judgement:

> The men who managed the Hospital combined good sense with good will and followed the principle enunciated by a special committee appointed in 1790 to investigate the Hospital's finances: 'that it is more consistent with the main Object of this Charity, and with the general Purpose both of Humanity and Policy, that a smaller number of Orphans should be kept well, than that a larger Number should be kept otherwise'.[21]

III

A Child's Eye View: The Early Days of the Foundling Hospital

What would it have felt like to grow up in the Foundling Hospital? In later chapters we are able to read personal accounts from foundlings looking back on their experiences, but in the early days we are dependent on documents from the archives describing the arrangements the governors put in place for the care of the children, and it is mainly these which will inform this chapter.

When babies were admitted to the Hospital, officials carefully noted their state of health and any distinguishing features, the clothes that they wore and any tokens that their mothers left with them. Most of the children brought little with them, and what they did bring was removed on arrival, partly as a symbol of their new status, but also for reasons of health and hygiene. The infants were washed and inspected to ensure that they were not infected, and then christened with a new name, regardless of the name that they came in with. The children would have remembered nothing of this first parting, although their mothers probably thought about it for the rest of their lives.

The governors had put a lot of thought into the clothes that the children should wear, both as babies and infants in their first five years in the country and when they returned to the Hospital. Well before the first child was received, the governors ordered sixty bundles of clothing, to be taken to the country with the nurse. Each child was to have:

> 4 biggins [a tight cap], 4 long stays, 4 caps, 4 neck-cloths, 4 shirts and 12 clouts, and also the following woollen clothing: a grey linsey mantle, a pair of grey linsey sleeves, 2 white bays [a type of baize of coarse wool] blankets, 2 rowlers [swaddling bands], 2 double pilches … and a grey linsey coat and petticoat and grey linsey bodice coat.[1]

By 1750 two pairs of stockings and a pair of shoes had been added to the list. The traditional practice of swathing infants tightly to prevent undue movement was to be followed, and the children were to be warmly but plainly clothed, with enough changes of clothing but no frills.

The fashion of the time was for infants to wear the same number of layers of clothing as older children and adults – two or three layers of head covering (a cap, biggin and headcloth, with ribbons for the girls), a shirt and clout, and a range of inner and outer clothing, in a combination of cotton, linen, wool, flannel, linsey and fustian.[2] The rollers were required to keep the blanket in place, not bind the child. Where the blanket was worn

with separate sleeves it was folded round the child. The
roller was tied round the outside to stop it all unrolling.
The last remnant of swaddling was dying a slow death.

The governors were much influenced in their approach
to infant care by a pamphlet written by Dr William
Cadogan, a fashionable London practitioner and later
to become chief honorary physician to the Hospital.
Entitled *An Essay upon Nursing, and the Management of
Children from Their Birth to Three Years of Age*, t he pamphlet was written as a letter to one of the governors, and
recommended less layers of clothing and less tight swaddling which he felt caused fits. Dr Cadogan said that
nurses think:

> a newborn Infant cannot be kept too warm; from
> the Prejudice they load and bind it with Flannels,
> Wrappers, Swathes, Stays etc commonly called Cloaths;
> which all together are almost equal it its own Weight;
> by which means a healthy Child in a Month's Time
> is made so tender and chilly it cannot bear the exter-
> nal Air … and the Child is so cramped by them, that
> its Bowels have not room, nor the Limbs and Liberty
> to act and exert themselves in the free easy manner
> they ought. This is a very hurtful Circumstance; for
> the Limbs that are not used will never be strong, and
> such tender Bodies cannot bear much Pressure … To
> which doubtless are owing the many Distortions and
> Deformities we meet with every where … [3]

Dr Cadogan called attention to the high death rate for
children under five, attacking the general practices at the

time and promoting a discussion of the proper methods of baby nurture. He recommended frequent changes of clothing for small children which 'would free them from Stinks and Sourenesses' and denounced the custom of giving newborn babies solid food:

> the general Practice is, as soon as a Child is born, to cram a Dab of Butter and Sugar down its Throat, a little Oil, Panada, Caudal, or some such unwholesome Mess. So that they set out wrong, and the Child stands a fair Chance of being made sick from that first Hour. It is the Custom of some to give a little roast Pig to an Infant; which it seems is to cure it of all the Mother's Longings.[4]

The enlightened view of Cadogan, on the other hand, was rather different. He urged the importance of breast-feeding, and advised that a child should have nothing but a mother's milk for the first three months, after which time he thought some additional food should be given. He recommended feeding at stated intervals, not the common practice of ten, twelve, or more times a day but no more than four times daily, and was emphatic that a child should not be weaned before 'a twelve-month'. Although wet-nursing was the approach that the governors adopted, there were also arguments in favour of dry nursing. One of the governors wrote a paper arguing of 'the danger of their [nurses] mental and bodily maladies being communicated to their sucklings', and pointed out that women might well neglect their own children in preference for being paid for suckling the foundlings.[5]

The Foundling Hospital was not short of advice, for it attracted many of the most eminent physicians of the day. The same year as Cadogan wrote his pamphlet, Sir Hans Sloane (the naturalist and collector, as well as physician to King George II and president of the Royal Society) wrote a long letter to the vice-president of the Hospital on the nursing of infants. He argued that two out of three infants will die if they are not breastfed, which he saw as the first and best remedy. If infants won't suck, Sloane recommended that they be given breast milk with a spoon. Well ahead of his time he argued that infants know what is good for them. He condemned the use of dry crusts of bread and chicken, pointing out that the first teeth do not appear until about eight months at which point weaning can begin, but proposed that breastfeeding can continue until two years. He saw great mischief from lack of breast milk, including gripes, green stools and an irritated gut.[6]

Knowing what we do today about the importance of relationships between children and their main carers in the first years of life, and of an environment that is supportive to their overall development, the placement of babies in the country with wet-nurses – or foster parents – is probably the best thing that could have happened to them. Although there were undoubtedly some children who were not as well treated as they might have been, the governors did all in their power to ensure that the nurses they selected were fit for the task, through their initial selection procedures; through the advice they were given on how to care for the children; and through the system of inspections both from the matron or the steward of the Hospital, as well as governors and the volunteer local inspectors such as Mr and Mrs William Hogarth. The nurses often lived close to each other, making inspection and support easier. For example, about forty nurse's cottages were in Chertsey, the majority of which were in easy reach of the inspector and the apothecary. The reports from the inspectors on the children they visited provide detailed evidence of the care with which these visits were taken. In June 1761, for example, John Tucker writes a long report of his visit to Watton on a Sunday where he visited twelve children 'all of whom I found in good health.' But he found fourteen 'very fine children, many of whom are but indifferently clothed which, I humbly apprehend, can't be much wonder'd at, when it is considered that the nurses there are in general very poor people' and six children who were not in a fit state to be moved as they were very weak.[7]

This was an extraordinarily advanced and child-centred system of inspection for the first children's charity to adopt and one that even today it is sometimes a struggle to maintain.

During their time in the country some children went to local dame schools but the majority were returned to the Hospital at the age of five. In many cases a strong bond had developed between the child and the foster mother and this parting is likely to have had a great impact on the young child. Occasionally the foster mothers prevailed upon the governors to allow them to keep the child and in time apprentice them, but this was the exception rather than the rule.

As the iron gates clanged behind the returning children, this was the last time they would be allowed into the outside world until they left the Foundling Hospital as apprentices. And it was now that the governors could begin on their quest of training the children to become useful citizens.

The children's health was the governors' first concern. The main diseases affecting children in the mid-eighteenth century were smallpox, distemper, itch (or scabies, a highly contagious rash) and scrofula (a tuberculous condition of the lymph glands, also known as the 'King's Evil'). But there were many other infectious diseases such as scarlet fever, dysentery, consumption, whooping cough and measles, as well as convulsions. During the general reception there was also the spread of venereal disease picked up from infected mothers before birth and passed on to the nurses through breast feeding. This was expensive for the hospital to treat, and painful for the nurses who suffered from both the disease and the treatment.

An early decision of the governors in 1743 was to inoculate children against smallpox – which was the cause of 10% of all deaths of children under three in London – and this was done on their arrival back from the country. This was a very forward looking decision, no doubt supported by Dr Cadogan and Dr Sloane, as even the smallpox hospitals for the poor did not inoculate children less than seven years of age. As a precaution, arrangements were also made for children suffering from infectious diseases to be cared for away from the Hospital, including a lease taken on the Coach and Horses Ale House. There were a range of additional preventative measures, including screening children on admission, destroying contaminated clothing, fumigation, general cleanliness, outdoor exercise, immersion in cold baths and other activities designed to build up the children's health and strength.

The governors also tried to anticipate accidents, directing that iron guards be placed round the fireplaces to prevent children from falling into the fire, and securing the window sashes in order to prevent children falling out. But as in any institution, not everything could be foreseen, and it was only after a boy was killed sliding down a banister that an iron rail with spikes attached at intervals was attached to every stair case in the hospital to discourage this temptation.

In addition to Dr Cadogan and Dr Sloane, the most notable physician was Dr Richard Mead, whose portrait still hangs in the Foundling Museum. It is unlikely that he would have personally attended his less well-off patients, but he gave the foundlings his personal attention. It was probably his views about the benefits of fresh air that started the policy of sending children to the country for their health. Dr John Mayo, physician to the Princess of Wales became the Hospital's physician at the end of the century and caused a notable stir by bringing charges against the matron in 1790, alleging that many of the diseases rampant among the children were attributable to her negligence of their diet, want of care for cleanliness and inadequate supervision of the nurses.[8] The children thus enjoyed, completely free of charge, the very best that the medical profession could offer.

The governors appear to have been aware of the link between disease and diet, noting that many children

became ill after returning from the country. Although
Dr Cadogan recommended to nurses in the country that
they fed children 'any kind of mellow Fruit, either raw,
stewed or baked; Roots of all sorts, and all the Produce of
the Kitchen Garden' we do not know if this advice was
followed. However we do know what the children ate
when they returned to the Foundling Hospital, as can be
seen from the table below, taken from the minutes of the
General Committee of 1762.[9]

	BREAKFAST	DINNER	SUPPER
Sunday	Bread and butter	Roast beef and greens	Milk porridge
Monday	Gruel	Potatoes or parsnips mashed with milk	Bread and milk
Tuesday	Milk porridge	Boiled beef and greens	Broth
Wednesday	Bread and milk	Stewed shins of beef and broth with herbs and roots	Milk porridge
Thursday	Gruel	Mutton and greens	Broth
Friday	Milk porridge	Stewed shins of beef and broth with herbs and roots	Bread and cheese
Saturday	Bread and milk	Rice pudding	Gruel

When the Foundling Hospital opened, the children only ate meat three times a week, but by 1762 it was increased to five despite its rising cost. There was no fish, eggs or poultry, but fresh vegetables were grown in the Hospital grounds, and there was a staple of bread. There is no mention of tea, which was strongly opposed by Jonas Hanway when he was a governor, nor of beer which was drunk regularly elsewhere – the children at Christ's Hospital for example drank beer for breakfast. There were also treats for special occasions, with plum puddings served on Christmas and Charter days and special buns served on Good Friday. McClure suggests that the foundlings enjoyed a more ample diet, and one of better quality and with more variety, than poor children who lived with their parents, pointing out that the governors took great pains to make certain that the quality of the food purchased was good, but also value for money.[10] However she also remarks that despite the attention, it is likely that the children were often malnourished by today's standards.

As far as clothing is concerned, when the children returned from the country they wore the Hospital's uniform, designed by Hogarth in 1745. A contemporary description tells us that:

> the Boys have only one garment which is made jacket fashion, of Yorkshire serge with a slip of red cloth across their shoulder; their shirts lapping over the Collar resembling a cape; their breeches hang loose a great way down their legs, instead of buttons is a slip of red cloth furbelowed. The Girls Petticoats are also

of Yorkshire Serge; and their stays are covered with the same, of which a slip turns back over their shoulders, like that of the boys, and is of the same colour. Their buff bib and apron are linen, the shift is gathered and drawn with bobbins, in the manner of a close tucker. The Boys and Girls hats are white, and tied round with red binding.[11]

The colour scheme of the uniform from the beginning, until it was discarded in 1946 shortly before the school was taken over in 1950, was brown (a symbol of poverty and humility) trimmed with red, and the governors ensured that it was made of sturdy woollen cloth (see illustrations 42 and 43). The children had to wear shoes and stockings, but they were not supplied with underwear. The children received new clothes each year before the annual meeting of the Court in May. And when both girls and boys left to serve their apprenticeships they were given a very adequate wardrobe of clothes to set them on their way.

As with schools today, the uniform was seen as an important way of encouraging solidarity and a sense of belonging to the institution, and it did of course save expense and arguments and envy between children. There was also a precedent in the blue coats and yellow breeches and stockings of Christ's Hospital, still referred to today as the Bluecoat School. But the uniform also set them apart from other children as it was only the charity schools that had uniforms, reducing the children to being part of a group of foundlings rather than individuals.

Although the children's physical health was the governors' highest initial priority, they were also concerned

that the children were well – but not too well – educated
and prepared for their role in life. The emphasis on
formal education for the middle and upper classes was an
emerging feature of the eighteenth century, but there was
as yet little understanding of developmental psychology
or the needs and interests of children who were expected
to behave as young adults from a young age. This is most
famously illustrated by Lord Chesterfield's letter to his
son, written in 1741:

> This is the last letter I shall write to you as a little boy,
> for tomorrow you will attain your ninth year, so that
> for the future I shall treat you as a youth. You must
> now commence a different course of life, a differ-
> ent course of studies. No more levity. Childish toys
> and playthings must be thrown aside, and your mind
> directed to serious objects. What was not unbecoming
> to a child would be disgraceful to a youth.[12]

Apart from charity schools, there was no publicly available education for the children of the poor, and indeed
many argued that education would be wasted on such
children and that it would make them unwilling to perform their servile tasks – thus undermining the whole
hierarchical structure of English society.

The opponents of this view felt that poor children
should be able to read the Bible and that they should be
taught to understand their subordinate place:

> To reconcile the lowest class of mankind to the
> fatigues of constant labour, and otherwise mortifying

thoughts of a servile employment, pains should be
taken to convince them, when young, that subor-
dination is necessary in society; that they ought to
submit to their masters or superiors in every thing
that is lawful; that nature has formed us for action; that
happiness does not consist in indolence, nor in the
possession of riches, nor in the gratification of sense,
nor in pomp and splendid equipage, but in habits of
industry and contentment, in temperance and frugal-
ity, and in the consciousness of doing our duty in the
station in which we are placed.[13]

At first the governors only wanted the children to read
and to be instructed in religious education. The sewing
and knitting mistresses taught both boys and girls from
aged three to six to read using a hornbook, a single sheet
containing the alphabet, the nine numbers and the Lord's
Prayer, used in England since the fifteenth century. The
boys started learning to write with the appointment in
1757 of a schoolmaster. They were split into two groups,
each one working in the Hospital and the grounds for
half a day and studying for the other half. The schoolmistress appointed for the girls at the same time was
expected to instruct the girls in reading, catechism, spinning, knitting and needlework in order to prepare them
to be useful servants.

The schoolmaster did away with hornbooks, instead
adopting battledores (alphabets pasted onto card) which
became very popular across the country ten years later.
Soon both boys and girls were being taught to write and
spell. As was the custom in schools for poor children,

the Bible was used as a reader, together with other religious texts. The children also had to learn the catechism, a task that was usually given to the reader appointed to preach in the chapel on Sundays. By the end of the century some boys were also learning arithmetic, so that in February 1800 the schoolmaster could report to the governors that of the ninety-five boys under his care from the age of five to fifteen, ten could read and write legibly, eight were learning arithmetic and five were fully qualified to go out with credit to be apprentices. Almost all of the boys who left the Hospital could write, at a time when only around 40% of the male population could sign their names. At the same time, all the girls who had gone out as apprentices could read the Bible and do needlework.

The attention that the governors gave to the girls' education was way ahead of its time, though it is not known whether this reflected Thomas Coram's views in a letter he wrote to a friend in Boston in 1737:

> [it] is an Evil amongst us here in England to think Girls having learning given them is not so very Material as for boys to have it. I think and say it is more Material, for Girls when they come to be Mothers will have the forming of their Childrens lives and if their Mothers be good or Bad the Children Generally take after them so that Giving Girls a virtuous Education is a vast Advantage to their Posterity as well as the Publick.[14]

Life was not all hard work however, and the governors allotted time for recreation, not just play for the fun of it of course, but play to build strong and healthy bodies. The boys were given bats and balls, tops and whips, and an outdoor play space to play in, but it would seem that the only recreation available to the girls was walking about the Hospital grounds chaperoned by their nurses and school mistresses.Religious instruction was a central part of their education, as all the reading matter was religious texts.

Perhaps the most unusual, and possibly the most uplifting part of the children's education was their musical instruction. In the early days the governors shared the commonly held view that poor children did not need to know how to sing or play instruments. Gradually, however, some of the blind children began to be taught the organ or singing in order that they could perform in the chapel, and during the 1760s one of the governors began to teach some of the children to sing psalms, hymns and anthems. By 1773 the General Committee were concluding that those children who could become proficient in music might 'be of great use to this Charity by adding to the Fund for the support thereof'. One of the governors was the blind musician and composer John Stanley, and it was likely that he pressed for the importance of music to the children, as well as playing the organ in the chapel on special occasions, writing hymns and anthems for the Hospital's use and conducting the annual performances of Handel's *Messiah*. The hymns sung in the chapel were also seen as educational, reminding the children that God's goodness had provided for them, for which they owed him gratitude and praise. But some were more explicit, as for example the *Hymn for the Children of the Foundling Hospital* by Dr John Hawkesworth:

> Left on the worlds bleak waste forlorn
> In sin conceiv'd, to sorrow born,
> By guilt and shame foredoom'd to share
> No mother's love, no father's care,
> No guide the devious maze to tread,
> Above no friendly shelter spread.[15]

One can only imagine how the children must have felt as they sang this on Sundays in the chapel, perhaps listened to by the visitors who flocked to the chapel each week who would have been urged by the governors 'that no familiar Notice may be taken of the Children, lest it encourage them to forget the lowness of their Station'. It seems unlikely that they would be allowed to forget.

In 1774 a proposal was put to the governors that the Foundling Hospital should establish a music school, similar to the conservatoires in Venice and Naples. It was argued that the school would pay its own way and bring in a profit to the Hospital, but despite initial enthusiasm the governors got cold feet and the idea was dropped:

> It was objected that music was an art of luxury, by no means requisite to life, or accessory to morality. These children were all meant to be educated as plain but essential members of the general community. They were to be trained up to useful purposes, with a singleness that would ward off all ambition for what was higher, and teach them to repay the benefit of

their support by cheerful labour. To stimulate them to superior views might mar the religious object of the charity, which was to nullify, rather than extinguish all disposition to pride, vice or voluptuousness.[16]

To get a feel for what life in the Hospital was like for the children on a daily basis, we can do no better than hear from Sir Thomas Bernard, then Treasurer, in 1799:

At the age of four years the children are returned to Hospital. They are then (if not sooner) inoculated and placed in the School, where they are gradually accustomed to regular and early habits of order and attention; the lesser children being occasionally let out to play during the school hours.

They rise at six in the summer and daylight in winter; part of them being employed before breakfast in dressing the younger children, in cleaning about the house, and the boys in working a forcing pump which supplies all the wards and every part of the Hospital abundantly with water. At half past seven they breakfast, and at half after eight go into school, where they continue, the boys till twelve, the girls a little later.

At one o'clock they dine, and return to school at two, and stay till four in the summer and in winter till dusk; except on Saturday when they have a half holiday. They are also instructed in singing the Foundling Hymns and anthems, and in their Catechism, and are occasionally employed in and about the house during play-hours. At six in the evening they sup, and at eight go to bed.

With regard to the employment of the boys, the little ones knit the stockings that are wanted for the children in the house; the elder boys, in their turn, work in the garden, and assist as servants in their own (the western) wing, and in working the pump, and cleaning the court-yard and Chapel. They are all taught, and make a proficiency in, reading, writing and accounts. Different occupations and manufacturers for the boys have been, at times, introduced into the Hospital. The last that has been tried with much effect and continuance, has been the spinning of worsted yarn. It was, however, attended with this inconvenience, that the boys who had been so employed, were not so much in request as apprentices, and were not placed out so speedily, or so well, as those whose writing, reading and accounts had been more attended to, and who had been occasionally employed about the house and garden. It should be explained that no apprentice fee is given with the children, and that the situation, in which the boys are very frequently placed, is with London shop keepers; to whom their being able to write and keep accounts of considerable importance; and it may be stated, as a general position, that 'youth being the school for life', that is the best occupation for young persons, which fits them most completely and effectually for their future duties in society; no profit being in general to be made from the labours of children before 12 or 13 years of age, which can compensate for their being less adapted, at that period, and during their future life, for useful and active employment in the situation for which they are intended. The item of manufacturers for the occupation of the boys has been, after some experience and consideration, given up at the Foundling.

The boys and girls are kept entirely separate. The girls are divided into three classes, under the care of three different mistresses, by whom they are instructed in needlework and reading. The elder girls are also employed in household work, and assist as servants in the kitchen, laundry and other rooms in the eastern wing of the Hospital. There is a considerable quantity of needlework taken in, and done for hire, at the Hospital; besides all the linen and female attire of the children, whether in the house or at nurse. The average annual produce of the girls' work (as near as can be estimated) is, from eleven to fourteen years, £2 13s 0d for each girl. Under the age of seven years, little or no value can be set upon their work …

No child is apprenticed except to an housekeeper; a very strict inquiry being previously made as to situation and character. No girl is apprenticed to an unmarried man, nor to a married man, unless the wife has seen the girl, and has expressed her concurrence in the application. Except in a few very particular cases, the girls are never apprenticed to any family that lets lodgings, nor unless there is an established servant regularly engaged in the house …

There was a period when the proportionate mortality in the Hospital had been very considerable and the children were neither healthy in constitution, nor promising in aspect; but that period is, I trust, entirely passed by. I question whether any public establishment, or even if private families, can shew better effects of care and attention in this respect, than what is exhibited in the Foundling Hospital. This improvement is to be attributed to several causes; – to the removal of an ill-placed infirmary to its present airy and healthy situation; to an increase of cleanliness in the children and in the house; and to some improvements in their diet, and (which I conceive to be very important to children) more unrestrained liberty during their hours of play and recreation. I repeat, with a confirmed and most satisfactory experience, what I have stated in the former instance, that an 'happier, a more healthy, or a more innocent collection of beings does not exist in the world, than is to be found within the walls of the Foundling Hospital'.[17]

Looking at the overall impression of what we can glean about the children's experiences during the first fifty years of the Foundling Hospital, and at the extent of poverty and the stigma of illegitimacy during this period, it can be argued that the children were in most respects a great deal better off than had they been brought up with their birth mothers. And it is clear from the mothers' petitions that they thought their children would have a better life in the Hospital than they could give them at home. During their formative first five years the children spent time in the country where they had a degree of freedom, individual care and close relationships that would have served them well as a foundation for later life. As they moved to the Foundling Hospital, they lost the freedom and the emotional attachment, but their physical care was well in advance of other poor children. The children's education prepared them for their station in life but, again, was ahead of its time in comparison to what was on offer in charity schools: it equipped both boys and girls with skills in reading and writing and some simple arithmetic, and they were given a sound foundation in religious instruction. And the overall environment of the Hospital, with its cleanliness and order, its pictures and its music, its large rooms and its extensive grounds, were way beyond what most children would have experienced wherever they grew up.

But we have no personal accounts from this period, and it seems unlikely that, in the words of Sir Thomas Bernard, the children really were happier and healthier than anyone in the world. The control, routine and isolation of the Foundling Hospital may have given them a sense of order, but it probably did little to prepare them for making decisions, forming relationships and surviving the hurly burly of life in the outside world. And they would never get away from the fact that they had been rejected by their parents, that their mother was seen as sinful, that they had no idea who they were, and that they had constantly been reminded throughout their childhood that they were illegitimate and inferior.

IV

HOGARTH AND HANDEL: CHARITY AND THE ARTS

A remarkable – and unique – aspect of the early days of England's first children's charity was the involvement of some of the country's leading artists. The mid-eighteenth century was a time of great philanthropy. As Hogarth's friend the novelist Henry Fielding wrote in 1752: 'Charity is in fact the very characteristic of this nation at this time – I believe we may challenge the whole world to parallel the examples which we have of late given of this sensible, this noble, this Christian virtue.'[1] Thomas Coram himself is an obvious example of this combination of Christian benevolence and hard-working zeal. The Foundling Hospital attracted a considerable amount of criticism as Coram struggled to get it established, and he was under constant pressure to prove to the public that it was a cause worth supporting. He needed to find ways of encouraging potential supporters to come into the building and see the good work at first hand. Whilst vulnerable children might be able to tug at the heart strings, sufficient space needed to be found to attract and entertain the great and the good. Jacobsen's design for the Foundling Hospital was plain and unostentatious, as befits an institution for abandoned children. But it was also spacious, and contained some fine rooms – notably the Court room and picture gallery – especially designed with fundraising events in mind.

One of Coram's many strokes of genius was to persuade so many leading eighteenth-century artists to support his fledgling charity. Foremost amongst these was William Hogarth, probably the most famous artist of his day and one who saw his involvement with the Hospital not only as a means of supporting an important cause – he was already a governor of St Bartholomew's Hospital and had done two large paintings for its staircase – but also as a way of increasing his own influence on British art and showing that he could paint better than European artists. It is not clear how and where Coram met Hogarth, but there appears to have been immediate empathy between the two men; both of whom had had difficult childhoods; both of whom had been brought up in poverty; and neither of whom had children of their own. Hogarth's first contribution to the Hospital was the engraving of a headpiece for the official fundraising letter in which a white-haired Thomas Coram, with the charter and seal under his arm, looks compassionately down on a group of weeping women, gesturing towards his new hospital. In the background boys wave at the ships out at sea, some are working on the land, and the girls are learning to spin (see illustration 1). It was all intended to assure potential donors that under the benign gaze of their founder, the children would be taught to be useful to society and would not get above their station.

It was also in these early weeks after the birth of the Foundling Hospital that Hogarth began his superb portrait of Thomas Coram.[2] He wanted to demonstrate that the British could paint portraits that were as good as the French, and he was furious at the way in which portrait painting was swayed by fashion. He wanted to paint a picture that was better than Van Dyck – and his biographer points out what an extraordinary landmark his portrait of Coram turned out to be. It was his first full-length painting and was the size that was normally reserved for the nobility rather than a commoner. Hogarth used all the standard baroque trappings of portraiture, surrounding him with symbols of his success, conveying the strength, colour and vigour of his subject.[3] Captain Coram looks justifiably proud, clutching the seal of the Hospital in one hand and his gloves in the other. The Royal Charter rests on the table, the globe of the world is at his feet, and his ships sail on the distant sea. But he also looks a little awkward and impatient to be getting on. His feet are not quite touching the ground, he is wearing his everyday thick red coat, his white hair is untidy and he is not wearing the wig that was customary in such portraits. Hogarth later wrote in his autobiography:

> The portrait that I painted with most pleasure and in which I particularly wished to excel was that of Captain Coram for the Foundling Hospital; and if I am so wretched an artist as my enemies assert, it is wonderful strange that this, which was one of the

first I painted the size of life, should stand the test of
twenty years competition and be generally thought
the best portrait in the place, notwithstanding the
best artists in the Kingdom executed all their talents
to vie with it.[4]

How right he was. In May 1740, when the governors
voted that sixty children be admitted as soon as possible, Hogarth gave the Hospital free of charge his great
full-length portrait of its founder (illustration 39). He also
donated £120 to the initial subscription, and painted a
shield to hang over the door of the Hatton Garden building in time for the arrival of the first children. He was
made a governor and attended fairly regularly for the
first two or three years, but he remained a supporter for
longer: designing the children's uniform in 1745, supervising wet-nurses with his wife Jane in Chiswick in the
1750s, and having children to visit his house. His wife
took one of the children as an apprentice to work in
their garden.

Hogarth also played a key role in encouraging his
fellow artists to join him in adorning the walls of the
new Hospital building at a time when there were very
limited opportunities for public art displays. Hogarth's
inspirational idea was to persuade the artists to donate
their paintings and sculptures to the Hospital, which
gave the artists the opportunity not just to be seen as
supporters of charity, but also to ensure that their work
was seen by other wealthy patrons. At a meeting of the
governors in 1746, at which Hogarth and the sculp-
tor Rysbrack were present, no less than fifteen artists

were reported as offering their support to the Hospital and all were immediately elected governors, including Francis Hayman, Joseph Highmore, Thomas Hudson and Allan Ramsay. Thomas Gainsborough and Joshua Reynolds also donated works, although they were not members of this committee, as did the marine painter Charles Brooking who gave what is considered to be his masterpiece. As the nineteenth-century Hospital secretary Brownlow notes: 'the donations in painting etc, the result of these meetings, increased and, being exhibited to the public, drew a daily crowd of spectators in their splendid equipages; and a visit to the Foundling became the most fashionable morning lounge in the Reign of George II.'[5]

Thus began regular meetings of artists who, in addition to donating paintings, had also begun to plan the establishment of a public academy in which to hang permanent exhibits and hold annual exhibitions. An annual meeting was held on 5 November each year between 1747 and 1759, when the major artists of the day would sit down to dinner at the Foundling Hospital. This was clearly an important gathering, with no less than 154 names of painters, sculptors, architects, engravers and other supporters (many of them doctors) listed for the dinner in 1757. In 1760 the first annual exhibition was held, with proceeds going to charity.[6] The paintings attracted large crowds, suggesting that there was a demand for a larger and more dedicated exhibition space, and in 1768 the Royal Academy was established with Sir Joshua Reynolds, another supporter of the Hospital, as its first president.

The arrival of new paintings was used as an opportunity to raise funds. For example on 1 April 1747 four
paintings were unveiled to the public:

> At the Foundling Hospital was an Entertainment,
> or publick dinner, of the Governors and other
> Gentlemen that had inclination – about 170 persons
> great benefactions given then towards the hospital – at
> the same time was seen the four paintings newly put
> up, done Gratis by four eminent painters – Hayman,
> Hogarth, Hymore and Wills – and by most people
> generally approved and commended, as works in his-
> tory painting in a higher degree of merit than has
> heretofore been done by English painters.[7]

Hogarth's painting *Moses Brought Before Pharoah's Daughter*
(illustration 44) was one of these four pictures of foundlings painted specifically for the walls of the Court Room,
where they can still be seen today. The religious theme of
these pictures, and particularly the two depicting the well-
known story of the foundling Moses being found in the
bulrushes by Pharoah's daughter and given to her attendant
(unbeknown to her, Moses' birth mother) to wet-nurse,
was also important in emphasising Christian charity.
The eight 'roundels' or small circular paintings still on
the walls of the Court Room are also worthy of note,
all painted on a single canvas and all depicting hospitals
of the day. These include the Foundling Hospital painted
by Richard Wilson (illustration 45) but the most interesting to art historians is probably Charterhouse as painted
by the young Gainsborough. The collection as a whole

illustrates the desire of the Foundling Hospital to command the same level of respect as the better established and older institutions.[8]

The Court Room, which has been restored as the centre piece of the Foundling Museum (illustration 47), is generally considered to be the best example in London of interior decoration during the 1740s. In addition to the four historical paintings and the eight roundels, the ornamental plasterwork is magnificent, as is the large fireplace surmounted by a bas-relief sculpture entitled *Charity and children engaged in navigation and husbandry* by John Michael Rysbrack, showing women breastfeeding babies in a landscape including children working in the fields and on ships – representing the useful trades for which foundlings were to be educated (illustration 10).[9] The room as a whole was designed by Hogarth to embody the central tenets of the Foundling Hospital – charity, altruism and the benevolent self-interest of the artists who supported it.

In 1750 another of Hogarth's paintings found its way to the walls of the Hospital. *The March of the Guards to Finchley* (illustration 46) had initially been painted for George II to celebrate the victory over the army of the Young Pretender in the Jacobite rebellion of 1745. The Young Pretender had landed in Scotland and marched as far south as Derby, much to the horror of the government in London. English guards are assembled at the Tottenham Court Turnpike before they proceed to Finchley to defend the city. The packed canvas is a riot of colour, confusion and contrasts – order and chaos, chastity and lust, drunkenness and sobriety. When the King saw the painting he is reported to have said 'I hate bainting and boetry: Neither the one nor the other ever did any good. Does the fellow mean to laugh at my guards?' When told that the picture was undoubtedly a burlesque, he asked 'What! A bainter burlesque a soldier. He deserves to be picketed for his insolence. Take his trumpery out of my sight.'[10] Hogarth promptly dedicated the painting to the King of Prussia, an encourager of the arts and sciences, and put it up for a lottery, giving the last 167 tickets to the Hospital. By chance one of these was the winning ticket, although Brownlow suggests that a lady actually had the winning ticket and gave it to Hogarth to give to the Hospital, rather than be seen to be supporting the Hospital herself. Hogarth duly gave the picture to the Hospital though he did say to the governors they were at liberty to dispose of the picture by auction if they wished. Very sensibly they decided to keep it.

As Browlow says, 'the Hospital had thus obtained from Hogarth a picture in each of the styles of painting in which he had attempted, and it may be said, without liability of contradiction, that the best specimens of those styles are within its walls.'[11]

The paintings were thus given in order both to draw attention to and raise money for the Foundling Hospital – and incidentally to publicise the work of those who painted them. The establishment of the picture gallery drew crowds to the hospitals who were encouraged to give financial as well as moral support to the charity. And many of the pictures were hung in the dining rooms, so that the children themselves benefited from their presence.

But it was not only the paintings that drew the crowds and helped to fill the coffers during the 1750s for, as any

choral singer or musician will know, George Frideric
Handel too became closely involved with the Foundling
Hospital. Handel's Covent Garden Lenten seasons were
well established by 1749 but he was also arranging a further schedule of concerts after Easter, including rehearsals
for his music for the Royal Fireworks in Vauxhall Gardens
on 22 April – so popular a concert that it caused a major
traffic jam on London Bridge, the only route across the
Thames. The full performance of the Fireworks music
was a week later, and it was after this that Handel attended
a meeting of the General Committee of the Foundling
Hospital and offered to give a performance of his music. It
is thought that he was introduced to the Hospital by John
Walsh the younger, a music printer and publisher who
was a governor and who published much of his music.[12]

Although the chapel was not completed until 1753,
governors had been using it for benefit concerts since
1749 as well as for christenings which always attracted a
large audience. Handel's first involvement was at a midday
charity concert on 27 May 1749 when he 'Generously
and Charitably offered a Performance of Vocal and
Instrumental Musick', the proceeds of which were to
be used for finishing the chapel. The concert had been
planned for a few days earlier but it was postponed at the
request of the Prince of Wales who wished to attend. The
Gentleman's Magazine describes the event:

> Saturday 27. The P and Prss of Wales, with a great
> number of persons of quality and distinction were at the
> chapel of the Founding's hospital; to hear several pieces
> of vocal and instrumental musick, compos'd by George

Frederick Handel, Esq; for the benefit of the foundation. 1. The musick for the late fireworks, and the anthem on the peace. 2. Select pieces from the oratorio of *Solomon,* relating to the dedication of the temple; and 3. Several pieces composed for the occasion, the words taken from scripture, and applicable to the charity, and its benefactors. There was no collection, but the tickets were at half a guinea, and the audience above a thousand.[13]

The pieces composed for the occasion included an anthem specially written for the occasion *Blessed are they that considereth the poor*, still sung today as the *Foundling Hospital Anthem*, and some parts of it also incorporated into *Messiah*. And so began a long and fruitful association between Handel and the Foundling Hospital. Like Coram and Hogarth, Handel loved children but had none of his own, and his own father had died just before his twelfth birthday. He would have also been influenced as a young man during his years at the University of Halle in Saxony by Professor Francke who had founded an orphanage that had become a model for similar establishments throughout Germany. He may well also have been inspired by the work of Antonio Vivaldi, who attracted crowds to hear his music at the Pieta orphanage in Venice in the 1730s where he was concert master.

Handel was elected a governor in May 1750 having at first turned the invitation down on the grounds that he would rather provide music than sit on committees. But on 1 May 1750 he conducted the first of many performances of *Messiah* that he was to give for the Hospital's benefit, to great critical and popular acclaim. The tickets for the event included a request that gentlemen would not wear their swords or ladies their hooped skirts, in order to make room for the large audience that was expected (see illustration 12). So many tickets were sold on the night that a second concert was arranged a fortnight later and a total of £969 7s raised for the Hospital. As a result of this success Handel accepted the governors' invitation to join them, and donated an organ to the chapel. *Messiah* became an annual event, and Handel himself conducted it for the last time in May 1754, virtually blind. He still attended every performance until two weeks before his death in April 1759. These performances raised £7,000 for the Hospital, a very considerable sum in the eighteenth century and recently estimated at a present-day equivalent of £750,000.

Shortly before Handel's death the governors presented a petition to parliament for an act vesting all rights in the oratorio solely in the Foundling Hospital. Handel was asked for his view but did not appear agreeable and nothing came of it. It is not surprising that he was not prepared to give away the rights, but given the popularity of the work – far more since his death than during his life – it could have brought very considerable riches to the charity. On his death Handel did however bequeath a fair copy of the score of *Messiah* to the Hospital together with his own conducting score of the *Foundling Hospital Anthem*, and both can be seen as part of the Handel exhibition at the Foundling Museum today. He also left behind a musical tradition which has continued to the present day of an annual Handel concert, usually held in February to commemorate the composer's birthday.

Heading to the subscription roll designed by William Hogarth.

2 *Captain Thomas Coram* by
B. Nebot, 1741.

3 Statue of Thomas Coram
outside the Foundling Museum
and Coram Family.

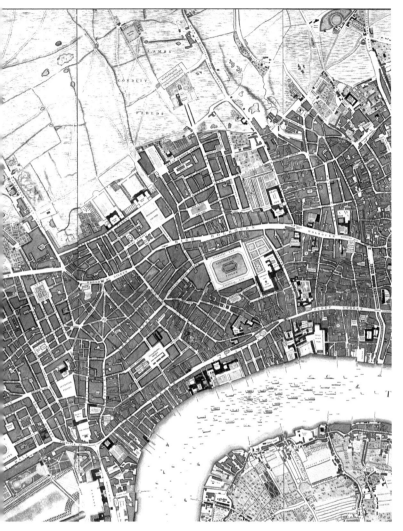

Detail from a map of London by John Rocque, 1746. The site of the Foundling Hospital was north of the northern edge of London.

5 *Admission of children to the Hospital by ballot* by Samuel Wale, 1749.

6 *The Foundling Hospital chapel looking west* by John Sanders, 1773.

7 Boys' dining room, photographed in the early 1900s.

8 *Girls' dining room* by John Sanders, 1773, showing the Hogarth portrait of Thomas Coram hanging to the right of the picture.

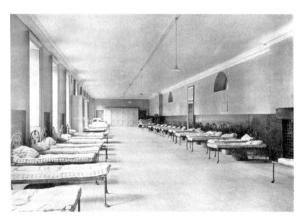

9 Boys' dormitory, west wing, photographed in the early 1900s.

Above: 11 Terracotta bust of George Frideric Handel by Louis-Francois Roubiliac, 1739.

Above: 10 The marble mantelpiece in the Court Room – *Charity and children engaged in navigation and husbandry* – by John Michael Rysbrack, 1745.

12 Invitation to the first performance of *Messiah* by George Frideric Handel, 1 May 1750.

FOUNDLING HOSPITAL
London

This is to Certify that _Esther Mayhew_ served the term
of her apprenticeship with honesty, sobriety, diligence and attention; and to the credit of this Hospital, where she
hath been preserved and educated.

In testimony whereof _Five_ Guineas and a Prayer Book have been presented to the
said _Esther Mayhew_ with this Testimonial of her good character, and the Seal of
this Corporation hath hereunto been affixed, in the presence of the Governors and Guardians whose names are
hereunto subscribed, this _9th_ day of _June_ in the year of our Lord One Thousand Eight hundred and _Fifty
five._

Sealed with the Seal of the Corporation, in the presence
of Three Members of the Committee, and attested by us.

13 Leaving certificate for apprentice Esther Mayhew, 1855.

14 The boys' band, Foundling Hospital, early 1900s.

15 Visitors watching children eat Sunday lunch, 1872. by J. Swain after H.T. Thomas, from *Illustrated London News* 7 December.

16 The boys' school room, Foundling Hospital early 1900s.

17 The girls' school room, Foundling Hospital, early 1900s.

18 The infants' school room, Foundling Hospital, early 1900s

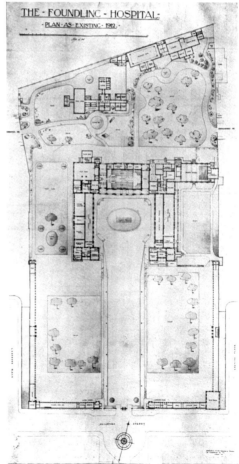

19 The Foundling Hospital, Guilford Street. Site plan 1912.

20 The Foundling Hospital, London, early 1900s.

21 A parade outside the Foundling Hospital, early 1900s.

22 The Duke of
Connaught, president
of the Foundling
Hospital, inspecting the
children, early 1900s.

23 The Foundling Hospital School at Berkhamsted, Hertfordshire, in the 1930s. It was later known as the Thomas Coram School and is now Ashlyns Comprehensive School.

Right: 24 Children marching out of the Foundling Hospital for the last time in 1926.

Below: 25 A foster mother in East Peckham, around 1900.

Left: 26 Choir practice, Foundling Hospital 1924.

Below: 27 The choir at a musical event in the Foundling Hospital chapel, 1920s.

28 The school band practising at camp 1926.

Above: 29 Summer camp – ring-a-roses 1926.

Right: 30 Summer camp – jam roley poley 1928.

Below: 31 Summer camp – boys on the trampoline.

32 Summer camp – boys washing.

33 Summer camp – girls in a sewing class 1926.

34 Summer camp – girls lining up for lunch, with the older girls taking care of the younger ones, 1928.

Right: 35 Summer camp – lunch time 1928.

Below: 36 Going to the circus from the Foundling Hospital, early 1900s.

37 Clowns at the Foundling Hospital, early 1900s.

38 Meal time at the Foundling Hospital School, Berkhamsted.

Right: 39 Portrait of *Captain Thomas Coram* by William Hogarth, 1740.

Below: 40 Engraving of view of the Foundling Hospital 1751.

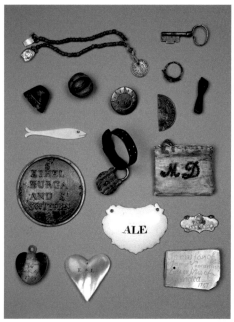

Left: 41 Tokens left by mothers with their babies.

Below left: 42 *A Foundling Boy* by Harold Copping 1914. The uniform had changed very little since Hogarth's day.

Below right: 43 *A Foundling Girl* Harold Copping, 1914.

Moses Brought Before Pharoah's daughter by William Hogarth, 1746.

The Foundling Hospital by Richard Wilson, 1746/50, one of eight roundels painted for the Court Room.

March of the Guards to Finchley by Wiliam Hogarth, 1749/50.

47 The Court room, photographed in 2004, showing Hogarth's and Hayman's paintings of the foundling Moses (see photographs 46 and 48)

48 *The Finding of The Infant Moses in the Bulrushes* by Francis Hayman, 1746.

49 *The Foundling Restored to its Mother* by Emma Brownlow King, 1858.

50 *The Christening* by Emma Brownlow King, 1863.

51 *Girls in the Chapel* by Sophia Anderson, 1877.

Sign at the entrance to ɔram's Fields in Guilford ʃeet, 2006.

53 Coram's Fields play area in 2006, with the original colonnades in the background.

54 Enjoying the annual Coram Family picnic for adoptive families.

55 Then Prime Minister Tony Blair and his wife Cher[...] meeting adoptive parents at Coram Family, 2000.

56 Children and parents at the Coram campus music event.

Parents and children in the Coram parents centre.

Children in the outside play area at the Thomas Coram children's centre, with the Foundling museum in the background.

Young people from Coram's education service celebrating their achievements, 2001.

60 Painting of the Foundling Museum, 40 Brunswick Square by Ann Usborne, w͟
the statue of Thomas Coram to the right.

61 *The Thomas Coram Story* by Rosa Branson, 2002.

No Goodnight Kiss:
Brownlow, Dickens and
the Nineteenth Century

The nineteenth century was a time of very considerable change in London. In the first thirty years of the
century the population trebled from 1 million to 3 million, as the city became the trade capital of the world,
industrialisation and urbanisation began to take hold,
and country dwellers flocked to the city to make their
fortune. By the middle of the century London was the
biggest and wealthiest city in the world, with a huge
buzz of traders, theatres, street performers and music
halls. And yet there was an inner core of poverty, disease,
homelessness, prostitution, crime and begging, as novelists such as Dickens, writing in the 1820s, illustrate so
vividly. As he wrote, 'The amount of crime, starvation
and nakedness and misery of every sort in the metropo-
lis surpasses all understanding'.

It was a century that witnessed a changing view of
philanthropy, as well as poverty on a huge scale. There
was a stronger emphasis on prevention and rehabilitation

rather than the relief of human suffering, influenced perhaps by the increasing population, industrialisation and urban growth, and the influence of utilitarianism. The reform of the Poor Law in the 1830s reflected this changing mood, as the legislation responded to the growing numbers of poor with its emphasis on self help, its attempt to limit expenditure by putting tighter constraints on how funding was accessed, and by further separating out the deserving from the undeserving poor. The Old Poor Laws were seen as encouraging bastardy by allowing mothers to name the fathers of their children, who could then abscond, leaving the mother to be supported by the parish. The 'Bastardy clauses' of the New Poor Law ruled that mothers alone should be made responsible for their illegitimate children. The only support for illegitimate infants was through the admission of their mother to the workhouse. But there were no facilities there to care for babies and as mothers were encouraged to work they were separated from their children. Although some of the Anglican dioceses were running homes with three-year training programmes to rescue 'fallen and penitent' women and place their children in an orphanage, it was not until 1895 that the Boards of Guardians of the workhouses received any instructions for dealing with their infant charges. Until then the care of children was left to the aged female inmates of the workhouse with little supervision – as we see in the opening chapters of Dickens' *Oliver Twist*.

It was also, of course, a century of major reform of the laws regarding child labour. Sir Robert Peel brought in the first act regulating child labour in the cotton industry in 1802, and after the Reform Act of 1832 Lord Ashley (later Earl of Shaftesbury), continued with attempts to try to limit the use of child labour. The Mines Act of 1842, for example, forbade the employment of women and children underground, and after many years of bitter opposition, Ashley's Bills to prevent the employment of children under nine in the cotton and woollen industries, to limit the working hours of people under eighteen to ten hours a day, and to forbid the employment of people under twenty-one on night work, were finally passed in 1847. It took a further twenty years to forbid the use of boys to climb up and sweep chimneys (as immortalised in Charles Kingsley's *Water Babies* published in 1863).

But perhaps the greatest influence on the changing views of philanthropy was the growth of the Evangelical movement. Their zeal and good works were in part responsible for the huge growth in the number of charitable institutions during the century – for example in 1861 there were some 640 charities in London, some 144 of them founded in the 1850s. But their values and priorities were different from those of Thomas Coram and his contemporaries. Where they had been moved by the physical presence of dying babies and the needs of their mothers, the new Evangelicals put the relief of spiritual destitution before the relief of physical distress. As the great reformer William Wilberforce put it 'The great business of our life [is] to secure our admission into heaven.'[1] The institutions that were inspired by the Evangelical movement had moral and religious ends as their prime objectives, and as McClure points out, few of their leaders were amongst the governors of the Foundling Hospital. If charity should reward the deserving, then this was unlikely to include bastards and foundlings. The movement did, however, lead directly and indirectly to the establishment of a number of other charities that are still very active today, amongst them the Royal Philanthropic Society (now Rainer), Barnardo's, the Home (now NCH) and the Waifs and Strays (now the Children's Society). We return to these later in the chapter.

Despite the many changes in the outside world, there were few significant changes to the regime of the Foundling Hospital in the nineteenth century from those established in the previous century. The daily life of the children remained much as it had in Sir Thomas Bernard's day, as can be seen from the following account by Charles Dickens who lived very close to the Hospital in Doughty Street during the 1840s. He took a close interest in the Hospital and was a regular attendant at the chapel, where he rented a pew for the Sunday services. Amongst the many characters in his novels are some who draw on Dickens' involvement with the Hospital: the foundling Oliver Twist (who, under the Old Poor Law, is farmed out from the workhouse until he is about eight), the less than ideal apprentice Tattycoram in *Little Dorrit* who grew up in the Foundling Hospital,[2] and Walter Wilding, the foundling who is reclaimed in *No Thoroughfare*.

But his most detailed account can be found in *Received a Blank Child* which was published as an article in *Household Words* in March 1853.[3] The title draws on the form that was filled in as each child was accepted into the Hospital:

> Hospital for the Maintenance and Education of exposed and Deserted Young Children.
>
> The [*blank*] day of [*blank*], received a [*blank*] child.

Dickens writes:

> This home of the blank children is by no means a blank place. It is a commodious roomy comfortable build-ing, … It stands in its own grounds, cosily surveying its own shady arcades, its own turf, and its own high trees … it preserves a warm, old fashioned, rich-relation kind of gravity, strongly indicative of Bank Stock. Its confidential servants have comfortable places. Its large rooms are wainscoted with the names of benefactors, set forth in goodly order like the tables of the law. Its broad staircases, with balustrades such as elephants might construct if they took to the building arts, not only lead to long dining-rooms, long bedroom galler-ies, long lavatories, long schoolrooms and lecture halls, for the blank children; but to other rooms, with listed doors and Turkey carpets, which the greatest English painters have lent their aid to adorn. In the halls of the blank children, the Guards for ever march to Finchley, under General Hogarth … In the Chapel of the blank children there is a noble organ, the gift of Handel.[4]

He then goes on to describe two mothers bringing their children to the Hospital, filling in the blank forms and leaving their children, numbers 20,563 and 20,564. Wet-nurses from Kent are waiting to take them, after their baptism (the new names having been a 'fruitful source of minor difficulty') back to the country with clothing and a note about payment – six pence a day and a clothing allowance of 14s a year for babies and 18s for four and five year-olds. Dickens then visits the infant school, where:

> … we found perhaps a hundred tiny boys and girls seated in hollow squares on the floor, like flower borders in a garden; their teachers walking to and fro in the paths between, sowing little seeds of alphabet and multiplication table broadcast between them. The sudden appearance of the Secretary and Matron, whom we accompanied, laid waste this little garden, as if by magic. The young shoots started up with their shrill "hooray!" twining round and shooting out of the legs and arms of the two officials with a very pleasant familiarity.

After a nice description of one small child trying on Dickens' hat ('with which an infant extinguished himself, to his great terror, evidently believing that he was lost to the world for ever') the party then proceeded to the end of the room to watch the band, which executed some difficult music with 'precision and spirit' and then sang Handel's Hallelujah chorus as loudly as a band of blacksmiths in Belper, accompanied by children beating drums, blowing dumb horns and trumpets and

flourishing wooden swords. Dickens comments that 'they
were all sensibly and comfortably clothed, and looked
healthy and happy.' He later concludes:

> Although we inspected the schoolrooms, the dor-
> mitories, the kitchen, the laundries, the pantries, the
> infirmary, and saw the four hundred boys and girls go
> through the ceremony of dining (a sort of military evo-
> lution in this asylum), and glanced at their school-life,
> we saw nothing so different from the best conducted
> charities in the general management, as to warrant our
> detaining the reader by describing them …
>
> Such is the home of the blank children, where they
> are trained out of their blank state to be useful enti-
> ties in life. It is rich, and it is likely enough that it has
> its blemishes … But from what we have seen of this
> establishment we have derived much satisfaction, and
> the good that is in it seems to have grown with its
> growth. Of the appearance, food, and lodging of the
> children any of our readers may judge for themselves
> after morning service any Sunday, when we think their
> objections will be limited to the respectable function-
> ary who presides over the boys' dinner, presenting such
> a very inflexible figure-head to so many young diges-
> tions, and smiting the table with his hammer with such
> prodigious emphasis; wherein it rather resembles the
> knock of the marble statue at Don Juan's door than the
> call of a human schoolmaster to grace after meat.

Other things too remained the same throughout the century. One of these was the policy of restoring – or more

accurately not restoring – children to their parents. Despite two well known paintings depicting foundlings being returned to their natural mothers – Francis Hayman's *The Finding of the Infant Moses in the Bulrushes* (illustration 44) and Emma Brownlow King's *The Foundling Restored to its Mother* (illustration 49) – very few mothers were able to reclaim their children. In December 1807 thirteen found-lings asked the governors for a relaxation in the rules so that mothers and children could 'preserve a mutual knowledge of each other'. [5] The governors resolved that 'The prayer is incompatible with the principles upon which the Institution was originally formed and cannot be acceded to'.

Petitions came fairly regularly to the governors, as for example this account of a couple who came before the General Committee on 6 April 1850:[6]

> Mary Jane John, who in her maiden name of Govin placed her child in this Hospital on 26th April 1843, attended with her husband Edward John and requested that the said child may be restored to her; and it appearing that Edward John is the father of the said child, and that the parties were married on Sunday last, and that the child is in good health within the walls of this Hospital,
>
> Ordered That the Secretary enquire into the charac-ter and respectability of Mr and Mrs John and of their ability to provide for the said child and report thereon.

The 17 November 1852 letter from the Secretary to Mrs Storer is not untypical of the governors' view that they were better able to care for children than were the birth parents:

> It is very natural that you should feel hurt at the deci-
> sion of the Governors, but you are mistaken as to the
> grounds of that decision. There is no charge against
> either your character or that of your husband: the
> simple matter is this – the Governors think they can
> provide for the boy's future welfare better than you
> can. You should recollect that you have other children,
> who may for aught we know stand in the way of the
> Boy; at any rate you ought to feel happy that so great
> an interest is taken in your son's well-being. The deci-
> sion of the committee is final.[7]

This view remained throughout the century, as is evident from the Annual Report of 1898 which states that
'many applications are received from persons anxious
to adopt children, but these are not entertained'. It is
not until the 1907 Annual Report that to this sentence
is added 'the committee reserving the right to restore
to their mothers upon being satisfied of their ability to
support them'.

Although not many mothers were reunited with their
children, the records contain large numbers of enquiries
as to their child's well-being, all of which were answered,
even if the child was never to know that the contact had
been made. Many of the letters include assurances that
the mother is now doing well, in line with the governors'
wishes – as for example this letter in March 1860 from
the House of Mercy near Windsor:

Frances is anxious to hear again of her child 'F' received Feb 21 1859 – will you kindly write to me here. I am sure that it will give you satisfaction to hear that the mother has conducted herself <u>perfectly</u> well and is now about to leave this house and enter a good situation as a nurse, where they have provided for her.

Another aspect of the Hospital's life that continued comparatively unchanged was the ongoing relationship between the governors and the foundlings that they apprenticed. As was noted in Chapter III, the governors took their responsibility very seriously for ensuring that the children for whom they had cared for so many years went on to lead useful lives. In 1806 the governors decided that no child would be apprenticed until they were fourteen, and by the middle of the century the girls were not apprenticed until they were sixteen. But the advice given to the foundlings as they went out into the world did not change, and is quoted by Dickens in *Received a Blank Child*. It is reproduced here in full as an insight into the intentions of the governors as they prepared their charges for their 'place' in the world, but mixed with the kind of advice that any parent of that time might have given their adolescent offspring as they prepared to leave home:

You are placed out Apprentice by the Governors of this Hospital. You were taken into it very young, quite helpless, forsaken, poor and deserted. Out of Charity you have been fed, clothed, and instructed; which many have wanted.

You have been taught to fear God: to love him, to be honest, careful, laborious and diligent. As you hope for Success in this World and Happiness in the next, you are to be mindful of what has been taught you. You are to behave honestly, justly, soberly, and carefully, in everything, to every body, and especially towards your Master and his family; and to execute all lawful commands with Industry, Cheerfulness, and good Manners.

You may find many temptations to do wickedly, when you are in the world; but by all means fly from them. Always speak the Truth. Though you may have done a wrong thing, you will, by sincere Confession, more easily obtain Forgiveness, than if by an obstinate Lie you make the fault the greater, and thereby deserve a far greater Punishment. Lying is the beginning of everything that is bad; and a Person used to it is never believed, esteemed or trusted.

Be not ashamed that you were bred in this Hospital. Own it; and say that it was through the good Providence of Almighty God, that you were taken Care of. Bless him for it.

Be constant in your Prayers, and going to Church; and avoid Gaming, Swearing, and all evil Discourses. By this means the Blessing of God will follow your honest Labours, and you may be happy; otherwise you will bring upon yourself Misery, Shame and Want.

The advice concludes by reminding the apprentices that every Easter, provided they are well behaved, they will receive a financial reward, and at the end of the apprenticeship a further sum of five guineas (see illustration 13).

Once the foundlings were apprenticed, the Secretary of the Hospital kept in regular touch with them, ensuring both that they were behaving as they should and that their masters were providing appropriate training. Sometimes the placement was terminated because the two could not get on together – as in the case of Mr Chambers and Jacob Blackhall, reported to the governors on 19 January 1850. The Secretary had asked a Mr van Heythusysen to attend the court at Highgate to speak on behalf of the apprentice Jacob in a summons taken out by Mr Chambers. Mr van Heythuysen's letter to the Secretary concludes:

> I recommend for the sake of the boy that the indentures be cancelled upon Chambers returning a proportionate part of the ten Pounds … It appeared that the boy was employed principally as a domestic servant, and not employed at his trade to the extent required by the Covenants in his Indentures.[8]

Sometimes the apprentice tells one story but his master another, as in the case of Mr Harding and Alexander Ramsey. On 25 November 1852 the Secretary writes to Mr Harding saying that the boy Alexander has complained of not being taught his trade:

> Whatever complaint you have to make against the boy (and there is no doubt you have reason to find fault with him) this is a very serious charge against <u>you</u>. He says that if you will teach him his business and not employ him in other work instead, he will be a

good lad for the future and do his duty. If you do not mutually agree on these points, the matter must be investigated by the magistrates and you must give me notice under the Indentures.

However, on 30 November after further investigation the Secretary writes to Alex Ramsey:

I find from a letter I have received from your master that you have made some false statements to me. He says that he <u>does</u> employ you at your trade, and the cause of the complaint between you arises out of your insulting and mischievous conduct, not only towards him but the neighbours also. If you do this, how can you expect to make Friends? … Keep to your work with attention and learn all you can. You have not long to serve and unless you pick up what you can in your trade you will be a vagabond on the face of the earth without a friend to help you. I am your well-wisher and have always been and therefore I speak plainly to you.[9]

We have seen in earlier Chapters that some of the blind children were trained to become musicians and earned a living through performing both in the Hospital and outside. It was not possible to place all foundlings as apprentices, and some of those who were disabled spent their whole life in the Hospital. Others came back for periods during their apprenticeship until the right placement was found. The General Committee minutes for 3 January 1821, for example, give the example of James

Martin, foundling no. 18891 who had been placed two years earlier with a Mr Tilt of Redland Farm in Dorking, but who had experienced severe fits. A letter from one of the governors suggested removing the boy to a smaller family, where he would get more attention for his health, and offered to try to find such a placement. Meanwhile James Martin was returned to the Hospital under the direction of the doctor so that his case could be considered.

And finally one of many examples where an avuncular but exasperated Secretary tries to keep one of his former charges from throwing away her opportunities and finishing up in the workhouse. On 17 January 1853 the Secretary writes to Elizabeth Morgan:

> I find you are again allowing the temper to get the better of your judgement, how is this? Will you never come to your senses? Your mistress tells me you can do well if you like! How wicked therefore must you be to allow these perverse dispositions to overpower you! If <u>sometimes</u> right, why not <u>always</u> so? It is clear that you can be good if you please and if you do not choose you must take all the consequences. Your mistress threatens to send you back to us: let me warn you against this; you have had already a taste of our reformatory; the next will be more severe, if indeed we do not throw you off altogether and send you to the workhouse. As your friend, I caution you as to the future; you have a kind mistress; do all in your power to please her and her daughter: and notwithstanding all that has passed, everything will be forgotten.[10]

It would appear that Elizabeth Morgan was not the only apprentice causing her mistress trouble. In June 1852 the Treasurer reported to the General Committee that he had recently had to enquire into a situation in which fourteen of the fifty-seven girls serving as apprentices had been prevented by their masters and mistresses from attending the Hospital at Easter to receive their customary awards, due to misconduct arising from their uncontrollable tempers. Having interviewed the matron, the schoolmistress and other members of staff he came to the view that, given the paramount duty of the staff being to 'instruct and guide the minds of the girls in a manner suitable to their present and future condition in life', the present staffing system had a 'want of union and singleness of purpose in the management of the girls, detrimental alike to their advancement and to the character of the Establishment.'[11] He proposed the appointment of a principal for the girls' school.

In July 1852 Miss Soley was duly elected principal of the girls' school and in September she submitted a report to the General Committee. She found the education of the girls far from satisfactory, with staff poorly trained and too much time taken with domestic duties. She was also concerned at the poor accommodation, where 196 girls were living in space designed for 103, and with insufficient lavatories and bathing facilities. She also found food was wasted. With regards the 'extraordinary instances of perversity and self-will' that she witnessed, her view was that the exercise of firmness and affection would change this over time, provided she could also 'make up to them the motherly care they have been deprived of by force of circumstances.'[12] The governors resolved to accept Miss Soley's report, including changes in the timetable, training of infant school teachers and sanitary reform. No reference is made to the motherly love.

There were other changes also to the children's education. A library was created in 1836 for the use of the older boys, and by the mid-century the schoolmasters and mistresses were teaching English grammar and geography as well as reading, writing, arithmetic and the catechism. Caning at the discretion of the schoolmasters and mistresses also came into use. The Secretary, Mr Brownlow, suggested in 1850 that tailoring as an occupation for the boys should be discontinued as it was injurious to their health, and from then on the clothes were made outside the school. Miss Soley had also suggested that the girls should no longer take in needlework and this was discontinued in 1861. A drawing master was appointed in 1862, and from 1868 some of the girls won academic distinctions outside the school and were being helped by the governors to go to training colleges. These developments were way ahead of their time, when we consider that universal primary education was not introduced until Forster's 1870 Education Act.

In 1847, also at the suggestion of Mr Brownlow, the governors instituted a Boys' Band, bought instruments and appointed a bandmaster. By 1853 boys were leaving the Hospital to join ships' bands in the Navy and in 1854 the band performed at the laying of the foundation stone of the Royal Free Hospital and at Drury Lane theatre for the Christmas pantomime. By 1856 the bandmaster of the Coldstream Guards was seeking recruits from the Hospital and in 1864 a new band room was erected – one of the few buildings of the original Foundling Hospital still standing today. As Nichols and Wray say in their *History of the Foundling Hospital*:

> it may perhaps be said that the formation of the Foundling Boys' Band was the most important development of the activities of the children during the nineteenth century. The practice has survived to the present day [1935] when it flourishes as it has done for nearly one hundred years. The majority of the boys who leave the Hospital today are enlisted into regimental bands, where they have gained many distinctions, one having recently won an Army Musical Scholarship at the Royal Academy of Music. A large number, after taking a special course of instruction at Kneller Hall [the army's band training school], have qualified and been appointed bandmasters.[13]

The health of the children also improved with the help of a new infirmary and the introduction, after experimental testing, of vaccinations rather than inoculations. The honorary surgeon recommended more healthy exercises and recreation for the children in the 1830s. The diet was improved, and is described by Nichols and Wray as 'exceptionally generous, and bears favourable comparison with that of any other institution in the country'[14] – although the 1840 report from the Select Committee on Public Charities remarked that 'few, if any, of the children brought up in this hospital attain an average height. … This fact is well known and admitted.'[15]

John Brownlow himself was perhaps the most outstanding member of staff in the Foundling Hospital during the middle years of the nineteenth century. As foundling no. 18607 he grew up in the care of the Hospital and in August 1814 he became a clerk in the Secretary's office. In June 1817 he was granted a salary of fifteen guineas a year and by 1818 he was allowed to dine at the officers' table. He was promoted to verger in March 1821 and by June 1828 was Treasurer's Clerk at a salary of £84 and allowed to reside outside the Hospital. He wrote *Hans Sloane: a Tale illustrating the history of the Foundling Hospital* in 1833 and in 1849 he was appointed Secretary on a salary of £460 a year, succeeding Morris Lievesley who died of cholera after fifty years in the job. When he retired due to ill health in 1872, the Court minutes recorded the governors' deeply felt thanks. The minutes refer to:

a service in various offices of the Hospital for the long period of fifty eight years, during which he has devoted himself to the discharge of his duties with an energy and zeal beyond all praise and to the great advantage of the Hospital and the objects of the charity. They earnestly hope that, in his retirement, he may find improved health and that full measure of ease and comfort which he has so well earned by a course of life singularly disinterested, benevolent and charitable.

His daughter Emma, who became Mrs Emma Brownlow King, also made a substantial contribution to the Hospital through her paintings, creating a series of images which convey the organisation in a very positive – and not entirely realistic – light. *The Foundling Restored to its Mother* for example, presents a contemporary version of Hogarth's painting of Moses with Pharaoh's daughter, suggesting that for a mother to reclaim a child was a rather more regular occurrence than was in fact the case (illustration 49). *The Christening* shows an orderly group of uniformed nurses bringing babies to the font to be baptised, under the watchful eye of a painting of Christ and a number of governors (colour plate 12).

Brownlow took enormous care in his dealings with current and past foundlings, birth parents and petitioners as demonstrated by the short extracts from his letters. His *Memoranda; or Chronicles of the Foundling Hospital, including Memoirs of Captain Coram* published in 1847 has already been referred to. Much of this work can be seen as a defence of the reputation of the Foundling Hospital and a refutation of the criticisms that followed discussion around the reform of the Poor Laws and the Hospital's own changing admissions policies.

The resolution passed in June 1801, that the principal object of the Foundling Hospital should be the maintenance and support of *illegitimate* children – a policy that continued into the twentieth century – was perhaps the greatest break with tradition in the nineteenth century. Although the governors had previously assumed that the foundlings were bastards, this was not always the case, and there had been no fixed rules around this issue. But from now on the Hospital was to be uniquely restricted to illegitimate children. No other foundling hospital or institution for the care of these children existed in England until much later in the century. Given the very high illegitimacy rate, and the fact that five children were turned away for every child admitted, this is perhaps surprising.

The governors set up systems for interviewing and reporting back to the committee on those applying for places, with particular scrutiny reserved for applications for legitimate children. For example, in 1807 the duke of Portland, president of the Hospital, applied for the admission of two children who had been born in Windsor Castle but whose mother had died. The application was initially turned down on the grounds that if their mother had died she could not benefit from the work of the charity – but on appeal the twins were eventually admitted.[16]

The new admissions system left itself open to criticism of abuse, as is evident from a case heard at the Mansion House in 1829 when it was alleged that 'only children of noble Lords and Honorable members are admitted to the Foundling, and the only way to get a child admitted is to send one or two hundred pounds.'[17] Although the governors refuted the criticism, it was an issue that was to rumble on throughout the century.

In 1836 a commission was appointed by parliament to inquire into how the larger charities in London set down the methods of admission then in operation. The report described the method of petition: the petitioner completed a form which was read to the governors, who then called in the petitioner and questioned her. The governors then made enquiries as to whether the petitioner's case was accurate, at which point (usually the next week)

she would be invited back and a decision would be made.
The report summarised:

> The most meritorious case, therefore, would be one
> in which a young woman, having no means of sub-
> sistence, except those derived from her own labour,
> and having no opulent relations, previously to com-
> mitting the offence bore an irreproachable character,
> but yielded to artful and long-continued seduction
> and an express promise of marriage; whose delivery
> took place in secret, and whose shame was known to
> only one or two persons, as, for example, the medi-
> cal attendant and a single relation; and, lastly whose
> employers and other persons were able and desirous
> to take her into their service, if enabled again to earn
> her livelihood by the reception of her child.[18]

The governors were asked to provide a random sample
of ten rejected and ten accepted petitioners to see how
far the policy was successful, and only two of the thirteen cases followed up approached the standard required.
The report (a copy of which is in the Foundling Hospital
archives covered with Brownlow's critical annotations),
goes on to condemn the earlier policy of general admissions for encouraging licentiousness, states that the new
policy is intended to prevent it, but then points out that
it does not succeed in doing so. The secrecy surrounding the admission is seen as encouraging illegitimacy,
educating the offspring of crime, and depriving the community of knowing the character of some of its members
– all similar arguments to those which had surrounded

Captain Coram's attempts to establish the Foundling Hospital 100 years earlier.

The name Foundling Hospital was clearly no longer accurate, as the children were now no longer orphans or foundlings. The governors sought the advice of the Attorney General and Solicitor General in 1849 as to whether they could change the name and were advised that they could, provided the legal title of 'the Hospital for the maintenance and education of exposed and deserted young children 'was not changed. Despite the recommendation that a short popular name be adopted, no change was made until nearly a century later.

Throughout the century, the Foundling Hospital found itself caught up in the debate about the relationship between philanthropy and the State. The Poor Law Reform Act of 1834 again emphasised the nature of the deserving poor and drew back the State's support for those who were 'undeserving' – and through its Bastardy Clauses acquitted unmarried fathers of any responsibility towards their offspring. The Hospital increased its attempts to distinguish between the deserving and undeserving supplicant, through its stress on sin and redemption and its focus on discipline and training of the 'rescued' children. Throughout the century the sermons preached in the Hospital chapel made the rescue of children through the mother's redemption their dominant theme.[19] But in supporting 'fallen women' it was seen as part of the Old Poor Law and as such came under attack from Francis Head, one of the Poor Law Commissioners. In his view the Foundling Hospital has become the epitome of 'this system of staff-fed charity' in spite of, not because of, its abolition of anonymous admission:

> Retaining its high-sounding name, it resolved that foundlings … should no longer be accepted; and … as babies really ought to have mothers, so from hence forward from none but their mothers should babies be received … we lately stood in the splendid square of this mistaken institution, we were politely informed by its secretary that we had before our eyes one of the topmost feathers in the cap of the British nation; that its immediate object was to seek out young women who had been seduced, and by accepting their off-spring, to give then what, with an air of triumph he called a SECOND CHANCE!![20]

The Hospital's secretary John Brownlow, and its Sunday morning preachers, did their best during the 1830s and 1840s to hold onto its eighteenth-century heritage as an innovative and forward looking charity in the face of critical reports and controversy over the New Poor Law. By the 1860s the Foundling Hospital was under further attack. In a paper on patterns and causes of illegitimacy in London delivered to the Royal Statistical Society, William Acton argued that single mothers should be supported in their efforts to keep their children through taking employment as wet-nurses to the middle classes. 'I think some such system … would be far better than the con-tinuance of the existing Foundling Hospital, which has ceased, I believe, to carry out the true intent and meaning of its founder.'[21] William Burke Ryan followed this up in his study of infanticide in 1862, asking whether the time had come for establishing a new and *genuine* Foundling Hospital,[22] and this was followed by further commentators from both the medical profession and the Church calling for institutions to provide help for mothers to bring up their children properly. Increasingly the Hospital was seen as raising a few select children at great expense, and reinforcing the very situation that it was intended to alleviate by preventing the unmarried mother from keeping her child.

Brownlow did his best to counter these criticisms, both through his own account of the Foundling Hospital published in 1847,[23] and through an anonymous pamphlet *Thoughts and Suggestions Having Reference to Infanticide* focusing on the critique of bastardy. He reinforces the intentions of the founder, and quotes from sermons in the chapel by the Revd Sydney Smith, evoking the biblical words of the communion service: 'No child drinks of our cup or eats of our bread whose reception, upon the whole, we are not certain to be more conducive than pernicious to the interest of religion and good morals, We hear no mother whom it would be merciless and shocking to turn away …'[24] Brownlow even refers to Fielding's profound knowledge of human nature and human action in his novel *Tom Jones*, quoting Mr Allworthy's reasons for sheltering and befriending the supposed mother of the little foundling. Efforts were also made by continuing to involve well-wishers and potential benefactors in the weekly chapel services where the sermons would reinforce the ethos of the Hospital, and the sight of the foundlings in chapel and going about their everyday lives was a testament to the work of the charity. Emma Brownlow King's paintings, noted earlier, may also have played their part in communicating the positive messages that the governors wanted.

The 1860s and 1870s saw a proliferation of philan- thropic institutions, largely set up by men with strong religious convictions who competed with each other as they sought to offer spiritual salvation and redemption to the poor and needy. Whilst none of them thought large institutions were the answer, they did share the view that children should be saved from their parents. Amongst these new charities were some of the best known today: Barnardo's, set up by Dr Barnardo in 1870; the Home, known today as NCH, established by Dr Stephenson in 1869; and the Waifs and Strays, now the Children's Society, set up by Edward Rudolf in 1881 – joining the Royal Philanthropic Society which had been set up in 1788. In one way or another, all of these charities were a response to the huge increase in child poverty, and their founders were focussed on rescuing children – moral reclamation coupled with huge energy, commitment and passion.

Children were seen as malleable, and so long as they could be removed from detrimental surroundings and pernicious influences, and placed in residential settings, all would be well. For example, Barnardo writes:

> Reclamatory efforts among the adult population of our slums are heavily and often fatally handicapped by the gathered strength of years of bad habits, and of vicious indulgence; the inertia of ignorance, of vice, of crime, is only with difficulty overborne by

the reforming forces brought to bear upon it. Hope, however, awakens when we cast our eyes upon *the Children*. Half our difficulties vanish when we have plastic material to work upon.[25]

A new environment, and religious training, was key. Children were to be kept apart from the contaminating influences of their parents.

In contrast to the continuing views of the governors of the Foundling Hospital, the new children's charities believed children should be part of a family, even if not their birth family, and they introduced small group homes and boarding out arrangements.[26] In this respect they were no doubt influenced by the report of A.J. Mundella who chaired the 1894 committee into Poor Law Schools who recommended boarding out as a method of care: 'the small details of everyday life help bring out the character of the child, and as it grows up enable it, though unconsciously, to develop self dependence, resourcefulness and thriftiness'.[27]

Sometimes the founders of these new charities were overzealous in the pursuit of their objectives. Dr Barnardo for example, 'kidnapped' or philanthropically abducted children whose parents were cruel or violent and by 1896 had appeared in court eighty-eight times for this offence. And in a well-meaning plan to provide children with a new start in life, the charities set up emigration schemes, first to Canada and later Australia and South Africa. In what Stroud[28] calls an unprecedented piece of social engineering, the Children's Society, or Waifs and Strays as it was then known, sent 73,000 children to Canada unaccompanied by their parents between 1869 and 1919. He argues that it was earnest, careful and well intentioned and that, in hindsight, it only failed in meeting the emotional needs of children. A legacy of the pioneering days of childcare was the thousands of children plucked from 'evil associations' who he argues, spent the rest of their lives searching for the people from whom they were plucked:

> The world of the waifs was a world of dullness and of unforgettable excitement; of simplicity and complexity; of kindness, harshness and abominable patronisation; of desolation and mischief; of security and insecurity. To a few it did lasting damage, to a few it brought unforgettable joy; to most it brought physical well-being but a lasting and indefinable uneasiness.

This policy continued well into the twentieth century and the repercussions until the end of that century, for both the children and the organisations concerned.

Before leaving the 1800s we hear from Hannah Brown, a foundling born in 1866 who wrote a first-hand account of her time in the Foundling Hospital which she left in 1881. Writing anonymously as 'A Foundling'[29] she creates an extraordinarily vivid picture of life in the Hospital in a book which she says she has written to expose a 'system which allows, and tends to encourage' unmarried mothers 'to abandon their offspring and give up all claim to them, which results in grievous wrong towards innocent children'.

She was brought to the Hospital at a few months old, and spent a happy early childhood in a cottage home –

she remarks that she never heard anyone speak ill of their 'mothers'. She was returned to London aged three where she was shocked by the regimentation – she says that she was never again addressed as a separate individual. She recounts one small child crying as her hair was cut off 'I'll tell my mother!' without realising that she had again lost a mother. The ordeal of the first Sunday led to her putting her tongue out in chapel, but 'such a spontaneous action never occurred again, I afterwards sank into the nonentity which the child who enters a Pauper Institution is bound to become. It was like the last flicker of a candle'. She paints a picture of the crowds who came to see the children (see illustration 15), and describes a meal time controlled by the mallet – perhaps used by the same person who upset Dickens' digestion twenty years earlier. At bedtime – fifty beds in a ward with a nurse at each end – there was no mother to kiss the children good night, and the nurses never attended to children who were crying.

Some of her fears are vividly described and must have been terrifying for a small child – the huge windows, dark at night without any curtains; the cold water for bath nights, when the nurses ducked the children's heads under the water; the monitors who punished small children who fidgeted in chapel; the dull routine and the strict teachers; the time she was shut in an upstairs garret for five days as a punishment for teasing the kitchen maid and messing about the with the milk churn. A teacher who greeted her with a kiss when she returned from a visit out is remembered with amazement as the only person who ever kissed her. What a contrast is painted with a three month visit back to the foster parents when

the Hospital is being repaired, and the fun and freedom
of playing with the six children of the foster family plus
the three foster children. She remembers the kind foster
father, the fun in the garden and the freedom of being
able to move around rooms without constraint. But how
painful it must have been for the foster parents who came
to visit on her return to Hospital to find that Hannah had
neither a word nor a smile for them – her spirit, she said,
had been broken.

Life improved a little as she got older, and by the age
of nine she was chosen by the nurse to be her maid and
then became maid for the infant school teacher. This
meant she didn't get turned out of doors before breakfast
into the freezing playground, and enjoyed evenings in the
teachers' room. She was later chosen to help the seamstress which freed her from schooling and the teacher
who she said hated her.

Another highlight was the choir. All children aged
nine attended choir practice three times a week. The
organist and choir master had been there for fifty years
and was 'a joy to listen to. What happiness we enjoyed
in this institution was chiefly centred round the grand
music, and the organist, whom it was our greatest wish to
please.' He treated the foundlings like any other children,
and Hannah delighted in a signed photo that he gave
her. The foundlings were given new toys once a year at
Michaelmas and Hannah remembers playing hopscotch,
trap bat and ball and croquet. The boys had a sports day
and a swimming pool, and tennis was introduced for
the girls just after she left. The highlights of her later
school days were annual visits to the home of one of the

governors, where there was a lot of space to run around and cakes for tea, and outings with the chaplain who took the older girls to Hampton Court and Windsor Castle.

Her apprenticeship as a domestic servant was very hard work and no one visited her from the Hospital during the two and a half years at her first job. Although her master and mistress were kind to her, the nurse to whom she reported was not, and her former teacher at the hospital was also unkind when she went back for her annual visit to the governors. 'And this is how the tragedy goes on' she comments, 'in regard to the lives of these "unwanted children" without a mother, friend or relative in the world. They are forced to submit to all the injustices and degradations which arise when they are thrown into the hands of complete strangers'. She was strongly of the view that 'Foundling Hospitals, whether they attain their professed and immediate object or not, are in every view hurtful to the State.' Without the men who make the laws on illegitimacy there would be no unmarried mothers, she concludes, and how can this system of separation help the mother? Every child is twice deprived of a mother – once at birth and once on being returned to the Hospital, and children are blighted for their whole life as they are forced to drink the cup of shame and humiliation for a wrong never committed. This is powerful stuff, which rings true today but is likely to have fallen on deaf ears when it was published.

Despite substantial changes in society, and the establishment of other charities to care for children whose parents were unable to do so, the nineteenth century was a relatively uneventful period in the history of the

Foundling Hospital. The policies and daily routines established in the previous century continued with little disruption along with some small improvements. The attention given to the children's health and education for example, whilst limited by today's standards, was nevertheless far in advance of what other poor children might have expected.

The changes to the admissions policy, so that only illegitimate children were admitted, and of those only children whose mothers could not otherwise find gainful employment, was perhaps the most significant difference. Every Annual Report of this period noted that:

> It should never be forgotten that this Institution, in addition to the maintenance and education of children, has another equally important object, namely the restoration to society and their friends of young persons of previously good character, and it is impossible duly to estimate the immense importance of this work.

But however well run the Hospital was, and however well the children were cared for, for children such as Hannah Brown there was no escaping the loss of two 'mothers' and the stigma and shame of illegitimacy – there was no emotional support and no goodnight kiss.

THE END OF AN ERA: THE FOUNDLING HOSPITAL IN THE TWENTIETH CENTURY

Whilst the nineteenth century may have been a period of relative calm and continuity in the affairs of the Foundling Hospital, the twentieth century was to see significant change. There would be two moves for the Hospital and the children; the sale of the London site; the gradual shift from residential to family based care; a broadening of focus in the charity's activities; two changes of name; and the establishment of a separate charity to care for and display the art treasures. This chapter looks at the changes during the first half of the twentieth century. The following two chapters describe first-hand experiences of growing up in the Hospital, and look at the current activities of what is today known as Coram Family.

The *Foundling Hospital Report and Accounts for the year 1913* illustrates the situation of the Foundling Hospital just before the outbreak of the First World War. This document is nearly identical in layout, and in much of the content, to annual reports produced during most of the nineteenth century and up until 1943.

The report starts with a summary of the history of the organisation, quoting at some length from the *Charity Commission Report* for 1836 which was noted in the previous chapter. Readers are then reminded of the rules of admission:

- Children can only be admitted upon the *personal* application of the mothers
- No application can be received previous to the birth of the child, or after it is *12 months old*
- No child can be admitted unless the committee is satisfied, after due enquiry, of the *previous good character* of the mother, and that the father has deserted it and the mother, and that the reception of the child will, in all probability, *be the means of replacing the mother in the course of virtue and the way of an honest livelihood*
- *No money is received for the admission of children.* [Their italics].

The statistical summary of children for whom the Hospital was caring during 1913 gives an interesting breakdown of children entering and leaving the Hospital, and conveys a similar pattern to other years:

Statistics for 1913

Children received under six months of age	47
Children received over six months of age	14
Sub-total: 61	

Girls placed out in domestic service   20
Boys enlisted in army bands   10
Boys sent to Navy League Sea Training Home   1
Boys emigrated to Canada   8
Boys sent to Farm preparatory to emigration   5
Children restored to their mothers   2
                                                  Sub-total: 46
Child died in the country, under one year   1
Children died in the country, under two years   2
Child died in St Bartholomew's Hospital, under nine   1
Child died in Children's Hospital,
            Gt Ormond Street, under eleven   1
                                                  Sub-total: 5
Children remaining in the Hospital 31 Dec 1913   372
Children remaining at nurse in the Kent district   151
Children remaining at nurse in the Surrey district   124
Children remaining at nurse in the Essex district   18
Children at Margate Hospital, Infirmaries etc   6
Apprentices and others partially maintained   7
                                                  Total: 678

Little had changed here over the previous 150 years
or more, with children starting their lives with foster
families in the vicinity of London, coming back to the
Hospital aged five, the boys moving on to apprenticeships or the armed services (often as bandsmen) at fifteen,
and the girls to domestic service at fourteen or fifteen.
Some 109 mothers' petitions were heard by the governors
during the year, just over half of which were accepted.
Only two children were returned to their mothers, but
it is reported that many applications were 'received from

persons anxious to adopt children, but these are not entertained, the committee reserving the right to restore children to their mothers upon being satisfied of their ability to support them.' From other accounts, the eight boys that emigrated to Canada after preparation on a training farm appear to have had some choice over their placements, unlike the many thousands of younger children that were sent abroad by children's charities from the late 1880s onwards. Most of these had no idea where or why they were going; what had happened to their birth parents (who were often told their children had died); and many were often treated very badly in their new homes.[1]

Seven of the apprentices were given some additional financial help to get them started out in life. Health records remained reasonably good, with a comparatively low death rate for the period, although a diphtheria outbreak accounts for most of the hospital admissions.

The report informs us that the schools were not under the government, but were inspected annually by one of HM Inspectors. The boys were instructed in swimming and there was a tailoring class for those who were to be apprenticed in that trade. The boys' band was still popular, with some 450 boys having enlisted into army bands since it was set up in 1854, and many went onto further study at Kneller Hall, the army band training centre. In 1913 there were seventy-five boys in infantry and cavalry bands serving all over the world.

Girls still assisted with the repair of clothing and bed and table linen, and made a large proportion of the children's clothing. The report tells us that they made 1,752 new garments, whilst the boys in the tailoring workshop made 308 garments in addition to mending their own clothes. The girls too were taught swimming and drilled by the headmistress. A large house adjoining the hospital had recently been purchased which took twenty of the older girls and trained them in cookery, laundry work, dress-making and other domestic economy subjects 'in order to fit them for their future life as Domestic Servants.'

Both boys and girls who had left the Hospital were required to produce an annual certificate of good con-duct from their employer until they were twenty-one and in return most received a reward, with a further gratuity of five guineas from the President at the annual Thanksgiving service. The report tells us that there were 122 boys and 84 girls who had left the Hospital but were still underage, and that those who could attend returned to the Hospital in May to receive the awards 'in accord-ance with their characters and proportionate to their length of service'. Seven boys and six girls attended the chapel service in June to mark the end of their appren-ticeship and receive their five guineas.

A Savings Bank had been established in 1867 to 'encourage provident habits among the former and pre-sent inmates of the Hospital', and a separate Benevolent Fund had been established as far back as 1809 to provide continuing support to foundlings who were not able to make their own way in the world.

The older boys and girls formed the chapel choir, along with six professional singers, and the Sunday morning service was open to the public, with a children's service in the afternoon.

The annual camp was organised in July and 118 boys spent 'a very enjoyable and instructive month under canvas' near Bognor Regis. (The girls also went to the camp in 1914, when the *Annual Report* remarked that 'It proved a great success; and the fresh air and change has had a marked effect upon the health of the children.')

In discussing the balance sheet (around £30,000 of income and expenditure), the governors pointed out that unlike other institutions the children were adopted into the Hospital and were chargeable until they were of age and sometimes for life 'should infirmity of mind or body prevent their being placed out in the world.' They estimated that the average cost per child per year, including those in the hospital and those in the country, was £34 11s 6d a year. The report notes that a heavy drain on resources was the upkeep of the 170-year-old buildings. It is also clear from the accounts that where once much of the income came from donations, the majority now came from rents for property.

The Foundling Hospital still had considerable support from the Establishment, with King George V as patron, the Duke of Connaught as President, five dukes and earls as vice-presidents, and sixty-six distinguished governors, plus all the members of the Privy Council who were *de facto* governors. The managing committee – including the president, vice-presidents, treasurer and some twenty-two governors – met weekly, a heavy burden on busy people.

There were only a small number of changes over the next few years. The grounds of the Hospital were occupied by troops during 1917, and although the War Office considered taking over the buildings in 1918 the governors protested and the plan was dropped. The Hospital avoided any direct bomb damage, and life went on much as usual for the children, with the Duke of Connaught inspecting (see illustrations 21 and 22) and listening to them singing in 1917 and the Queen visiting and seeing the children at work in their classrooms in 1918. Reginald Nichols (one of the authors of *The History of the Foundling Hospital*) was appointed Secretary (the most senior paid official), having been assistant secretary since 1908, replacing Mr Wintle who had been in the job for over forty-five years. By 1918 it was reported that 'the mothers of the children may enquire as to their health as often as they wish and may send presents to the children',[2] and although some began to do so, some of the children quoted in the next Chapter were not aware of who the presents were from.

With the passing of the Education Act in 1918, the Foundling Hospital began to be out of step with changes in the outside world. Although the schools within the Hospital had been inspected every year, this was not an official government inspection, and as a non-state school it began to become more difficult to recruit teachers, particularly when, under the new act, teachers were provided with state pensions. The governors therefore applied to the Board of Education to be inspected under the Education Act, and for their teachers to have the benefits of pensions.[3] The Board of Education duly inspected the following year, but was not prepared to recognise the Foundling Hospital within the terms of the act unless the governors applied to be recognised as an Elementary School, giving the London County

Council the opportunity to maintain the schools. This they duly did, but the LCC decided they were not prepared to maintain the schools.

By 1920 there was a serious financial deficit due to rising costs and the number of children admitted had to be reduced. One way of reducing costs would have been to return some of the children to their foster parents, and indeed the Annual Report notes that many foster mothers applied to adopt children that they had brought up and cared for during their early years. But after careful consideration by governors and medical staff the governors decided:

> on account of the risk of infection and for other reasons that they were not able to consent to the suggestion; at the same time they recognise very fully the affection of the Foster Mothers and the great benefit the children derive from the association with them in the country. In many cases the attachments formed in early childhood continue in after life, and many of the children have married relatives of the foster mothers.[4]

This must have been a difficult time for the governors whose policies were coming under fire from a number of different directions. In the first Thanksgiving service since the First World War, in 1921, the Bishop of Birmingham argued that the Foundling Hospital was still needed, for twice as many illegitimate as legitimate children die, but 'My belief is so strong in the parent being the natural and proper teacher about God and Jesus Christ that I would never remove from touch with its mother any illegitimate child'. He said that he was glad that mothers could send presents and children could be restored, for 'However kindly the child may be treated in the institution, however homely you may make the surroundings, the little person will want the sense of someone lovingly interested in its welfare.'[5]

In the same year Dr Bruce Low from the Ministry of Health wrote a very critical report on the Hospital following an outbreak of scarlet fever. He said that the methods of bringing up foundlings were out of date, that none of the staff had any knowledge of child welfare, and that the children had 'an institutional appearance and appear dull witted … The children appear to behave mechanically and the natural buoyancy of spirits of a young child seem to be totally absent.'[6] The Hospital medical officer replied with an angry list of inaccuracies, and Colonel Nichols wrote and complained to the Ministry of Health, saying that the governors were planning to move the children out of London.

Costs were by now increasing faster than income, and the impact of the First World War exacerbated an already difficult situation. For some years the governors had indeed been trying to sell the site and move the children away from what had increasingly become an inner-city area. In this respect they were following the precedent created by Charterhouse School which left London for Godalming, and Christ's Hospital which left London for Horsham, both feeling that the children would be healthier in the country.

Plans to sell the Hospital site alone to the Great Northern Railway for a terminus and then to London University fell through, but in 1922 a property developer offered to buy the whole of the Hospital Estate – some fifty-six acres of Bloomsbury and Holborn. Negotiations were protracted, but eventually a contract was agreed in 1925 for the sale of the whole Estate. When it became known that the objective of the purchasers was to transfer Covent Garden market to the site, there was huge opposition from local residents, many of whom were very distinguished individuals who formed themselves into The Foundling Estate Protection Association in order to preserve the estate as an open space for the public. They were unable to raise the funds required and a voluntary Children's Playcentres committee was formed, with Janet Trevelyan as chair (wife of the historian G.M. Trevelyan and daughter of Mary Ward who founded the Mary Ward Settlement in Queen's Square), to raise funds to purchase the site for preservation as a children's playground. This was eventually successful, with the help of Lord Rothermere and funding from the London County Council, and so the large children's play area known today as Coram's Fields (where no adult is allowed unless accompanied by a child), was born. The Hospital governors bought back the northern portion of the site in order to develop its infant welfare work for babies coming into the Hospital – in the area that is today the headquarters of the charity, now called Coram Family.

The King and Queen and the duke of Connaught came to pay a farewell visit, and again the governors discussed a proposal to change the name of the Foundling Hospital to Coram's School – but again they rejected the proposal.

The governors could not, of course, move out of the Hospital site until they had found alternative accommodation for the children. In the short-term they were able to buy St Anne's Schools at Redhill, where the children moved to in 1926 after a three-month summer camp at Pangbourne until the new school was ready for them.

Finding a permanent site was more difficult. The disadvantage of leaving London would be that the public might forget about the charity, and it is clear that the Sunday chapel services had been successful in maintaining the charity's presence in the capital and in engaging the interest of the many distinguished people who became governors. The governors therefore started looking for:

> a site in the country, with an area of not less than 150 acres; not more than 40 miles from London; not on clay soil but on gravel if possible; and also with main drainage, company's water, gas and electric light; a site with an altitude not less than 200 feet above sea-level, near a village and main railway station, and preferably near a main thoroughfare and within easy access of London.[7]

After inspecting a number of properties, including Ashridge in Hertfordshire, Claremont in Surrey and Stowe in Buckinghamshire, a site was purchased at Berkhamsted.

The Berkhamsted site comprised 200 acres of land overlooking the town of Berkhamsted, on the borders of Hertfordshire and Buckinghamshire. The governors visited a lot of institutions to inform their decision of what to build, from country homes where children were housed in cottages with a foster mother to 'barrack schools' where they were all housed in one large building. They chose the large building, but broken up into smaller sections than the London hospital, with separate dormitories for twenty-five children each, with two dormitories to be designated as a 'House'. In addition, the school was to have a chapel, a concert hall, dining room, swimming pool and gymnasium.

The foundation stone of the building, designed by John Shepherd and closely based on the original Jacobsen design of the Foundling Hospital, was laid in 1933. In July 1935, two years later and almost 200 years after the opening of the Foundling Hospital, some 300 children transferred from Redhill to Berkhamsted, preceded by their band and welcomed by the governors and the local council, with Handel's 'He shall feed his flock' from *Messiah* being played on the organ that had been Handel's gift to the Hospital. Nichols and Wray comment:

> Those who remembered the schools when in Bloomsbury could scarcely fail to have been moved on seeing the children again permanently settled in buildings reminiscent in so many details of Coram's original foundation; buildings which maintained not only the traditions but incorporated many actual

portions such as the pulpit, stained glass windows, old oak staircase and stone obelisks.

It was appropriate that the mortal remains of the founder should have preceded the children a few days previously to find a permanent resting place beneath the altar in the children's chapel.[8]

The grounds and the buildings gave the children considerably more space than they had had in London, but the situation was more isolated, as the site was tucked away on the edge of the town and there were few passers-by and less visits from the governors and potential supporters (see illustration 23).

Meanwhile, back in London, the governors decided to develop the section of the original site that they had purchased back from Lord Rothermere. They sought an extension of their original objects through the 1936 Foundling Hospital Act, broadening the objectives to include work in education and the welfare of children in need, and they proceeded to build an infant welfare centre, day nursery and nursery school – a building which was recently refurbished and is now the headquarters of Coram Family. The governors also took over responsibility for the Cross Roads Club, a hostel for expectant mothers and mothers and babies. At this point, they were also running a holiday play centre, a canteen for children, and they had opened up the swimming pool to local children.

St Leonards Nursery School, a nursery taking eighty young children from poor and crowded homes, was already on the site. The former pupils of St Leonards

School in St Andrews in Scotland had set it up in 1930 in the old infirmary building:

> There was great poverty and distress in the area in the early 1930s owing to the slump and unemployment. About a third of the children had to be bathed and dressed in school clothes when they arrived. Though the charge for school meals was only four pence a day, which included breakfast, milk and biscuits, elevenses, milk, midday meal, and milk and biscuits for tea before leaving, even so 25% had free or reduced price meals. Dirty heads were quite common. Girls of St Leonards School made clothes and aprons for the children who needed them.[9]

St Leonards had originally hoped to build a nursery school on the site, but somewhat to their dismay the Foundling Hospital governors preferred to include the nursery school in their own new centre. The nursery school and the Foundling Hospital's day nursery (also opened in 1930 to care for children under five to enable their mothers to work), were to be on the ground floor, and on the first floor a residential nursery to take children admitted to the Hospital as they were waiting to be placed with foster parents, plus a child care training centre. The training centre – known as the Thomas Coram Child Care Centre and which opened in 1939 – was an interesting forerunner of today's work on the Coram Community Campus. The day nursery, residential nursery and nursery school provided excellent opportunities for students to study young children as they trained to become teachers, social workers or nurses, and the childcare courses offered a mixture of theory and practice under the expert eyes of Freda Hawtrey, former principal of Avery Hill Training College, and the legendary Susan Isaacs, at that time Head of Child Development at London University.

As plans proceeded for the building of the Child Welfare Building, which was to replace the old infirmary building, the governors were also going ahead with plans to rebuild 40 Brunswick Square as their London headquarters, a base from where they would admit new children, and where they could house the Court Room and Picture Gallery, which had been carefully dismantled when the Foundling Hospital had been pulled down. Both buildings were completed just before the outbreak of the Second World War, and were opened by Queen Elizabeth in March 1939, before children, staff and pictures were evacuated to the comparative safety of Berkhamsted.

Back at Berkhamsted there was not a great deal of change before the Second World War, and indeed a child entering the Foundling Hospital at the age of five in 1942 would have seen little difference in the daily life from one entering twenty years earlier. 'Harsh discipline, long hours outside in the playground regardless of weather, hours in the playroom sitting round the outside looking at each other, and marching in threes around the school led by the school band.'[10] Each year, one or two of the brighter girls were given the opportunity of escaping from the prospect of a career in domestic service by going to Camden High School – providing they were 'very well behaved', an arrangement set up when the Foundling Hospital was still in London. The boys mainly continued to go into the army, many still as band boys. The school was usually very successful in the army apprentices' examinations. In 1939 for example, five out of six boys passed when 1,000 candidates throughout the country competed for 200 places.[11]

The accommodation for the children may have been more spacious at Berkhamsted than it had in London, but the close links between the governors and the school were weakened: where governors had had daily contact with the children in London, they now had to rely on the Secretary who lived in the school grounds, for information. Some of the staff – and indeed the governors – having served the Hospital for long periods were getting a little out of touch with the need to change. The minute books record increasing indiscipline during this period, perhaps because some of the younger and better staff were called up to serve in the war, and it is clear from the accounts in the next chapter that there was a good deal of bullying and general unhappiness – particularly under one long-serving headmaster who retired in 1943. Although many who attended boarding schools at that time also found the regime tough, they at least were able to go home in the holidays and did not have to live with the stigma of illegitimacy and rejection.

Although an incendiary device fell on the roof of 40 Brunswick Square during the war (successfully dealt with by the caretaker, who was awarded a gratuity of £1 for his bravery), Berkhamsted sustained no bomb damage – which is just as well as the number of children on the books in 1941 remained as high as at any time since the days of open admissions in the mid-eighteenth century. Air-raid shelters were provided for the children, and three acres of playing fields were dug up and planted with vegetables as part of the 'dig for victory' campaign.

Change came comparatively quickly after the end of the war. In response to the huge number of children evacuated and living apart from their parents during the war, the government established a committee in 1945 under the chairmanship of Dame Myra Curtis to:

> inquire into existing methods of providing for children who from loss of parents or from any cause whatever are deprived of a normal home life with their parents or relatives; and to consider what further measures should be taken to ensure that these children are brought up under conditions best calculated to compensate them for the lack of parental care.[12]

The largest group of children were those maintained by local authorities under the Poor Law Act, but there were also thousands of children boarded out in workhouses and in a wide variety of residential homes. While there is no evidence that the report had the Foundling Hospital in mind, it is particularly critical of residential homes which kept children shut off from the outside world in the hands of untrained staff. Homes that failed were those that 'gave too much weight to traditional methods and too little to the modern outlook in childcare'. Large buildings necessitated mass methods, the report said, where physical care was often reasonable but the children tended to be listless and apathetic. Dressing children alike created the stigma of the 'charity child', and the best meals were not served at long tables. Children often had little privacy and did not possess their own toys, nor were they able to join in the life of the local community.

The report concluded that a deprived child needs a home or substitute home which supplies affection and personal interest; understanding of his defects; care for his future; respect of his personality and regard for his self esteem; stability, opportunity to make the best of his ability and aptitude; and a share in the common life of a small group of people. If a child is illegitimate, every effort should be made to keep the child at home with its mother. The report favoured adoption – but only through registered adoption agencies – and felt that boarding out, or fostering, was the next best option. It recommended the phasing out of residential institutions, which have a tendency:

> to lack of interest in the child as an individual and to remote and impersonal relations … Many children in homes are physically better cared for as regards food, clothing and accommodation than they would have been if they had remained with their parents … we are convinced by what we have seen and heard … that on the human and emotional side they continually feel the lack of affection and personal interest.[13]

The Curtis Report also included recommendations on staffing and on dress (there should not be a uniform that distinguishes the children from other children). It recognised that certain behaviours such as bed wetting were linked to insecurity and should not be punished. It also advised that care should be taken to avoid stereotypical placing of boys as farm hands or army bandsmen, and said that 'an assumption that domestic work is the only outlet for girls has been far too prevalent'.

The report had been informed by the views of some of the foremost childcare experts of the day including: the psychologist Susan Isaacs who was also involved in the Thomas Coram Childcare Centre; the eminent child psychiatrist John Bowlby; and the equally eminent paediatrician and psychiatrist Donald Winnicott. These individuals have all had a profound influence on our understanding of a child's need for close and secure attachments if they are to grow into fully functional adults, and the importance of parents in providing these for their children. The report provided a blueprint for the 1948 Children Act which gave local authorities the responsibility for setting up children's departments and created a new framework within which specialist social workers would work with the families of vulnerable children under the direction of children's officers.

During the 1940s the Foundling Hospital had come under increasing pressure from former pupils such as Hannah Brown (whose book we drew on in Chapter V), and some foster mothers who asked to be allowed to care for their foundling children in the school holidays. In 1945, in response to pressure from foster parents, the children were allowed to visit their foster homes for three weeks at Easter, and soon going home for the holidays became a regular practice. But during the debates in parliament on the Children Bill, critical articles appeared in the press. The Home Office, responsible for children's issues under the new act, became involved when a birth mother who wanted to reclaim her nine year-old daughter went to see a senior official there. The Home Office questioned the continuing practice of changing a child's name on admission to the Hospital, and the wording of the receipt which was still headed – as it had been in Dickens day – 'Hospital for the maintenance and education of exposed and deserted young children'. As the Home Office letter says, 'Does this not seem rather hard when applied to a case where a young mother chooses to ask the Schools to receive her child as the best she can do for it and when afterwards she enquires regularly about its welfare although she has never seen it since?'[14]

In March 1948 the governors decided to retain the mother's name and to change the receipt, whilst pointing out that some mothers did in fact want the name changed. The letter from the Secretary, Colonel Nichols, referred to attempts to get Somerset House to produce shortened birth certificates for those leaving the Hospital – an action taken by the governors after they came under sustained pressure to do so from a petition signed by forty-eight old boys and girls who were still having to live with the stigma of the Foundling Hospital certificates. Nichols also says that the governors were changing the rules so that mothers could visit their children. He concluded his letter by saying that these changes were some of the most important in the history of the Institution and:

it would be appreciated if the Home Secretary would refer to the matter in the House when the Children Bill comes up for debate. The governors are anxious that the public should realise, as is the fact, that we have made the decision of our own accord in view of changing social conditions and knowledge of children and not as a result of publicity given to the matter in the House of Lords of to pressure from higher authority.[15]

Changes came quickly after this. In 1953 an Act of Parliament permitted the Registrar General to issue former pupils with a short birth certificate in their Hospital name. During the late 1940s and 1950s efforts were made to trace mothers, and to reintroduce mothers to their children. Given the governors' commitment to the mothers to keep their names secret, this could only be done in the first instance by a press appeal in the *Daily Telegraph* which, not surprisingly, did not attract many responses. After an appeal from former pupils, a member of staff was appointed to contact mothers to see if they wished to meet up with their children, although at that time there was little recognition of the complexity of introducing birth mothers to their children and the range of emotions that this would evoke. The staff member reported in 1952 that of fifty-one cases completed, twenty-seven mothers were going to meet their children, seven had refused and thirteen were dead or could not be traced.

In 1954 the name Foundling Hospital was finally changed – almost 100 years after a change of name was first proposed – to the Thomas Coram Foundation for Children. The school in Berkhamsted had already become The Thomas Coram School, and there were more changes to how the school was organised. The children were already organised into four houses – Coram, Handel, Hogarth and Dickens – and the boys were now given opportunities for higher education. In 1949 the school had been organised into a primary and secondary department and for the first time boys and girls were educated in mixed classes. And in 1947 the Old Coram Association was set up to provide an opportunity for former pupils to keep in touch with each other.

But gradually the numbers in the school reduced, due to financial difficulties and the challenges of finding sufficient foster parents, both for new babies coming into the institution and for the older children who were now going home for the holidays. There were staffing shortages and in 1948 the governors asked Hertfordshire County Council to take over responsibility for the education at the school. The residential part of the school retained its independence under the Coram governors, a proposal warmly welcomed by the Home Office. The standard of teaching began to improve, particularly as younger teachers came in after the war, and the children began to be given more freedom to leave the grounds and visit Berkhamsted.

In 1950 the announcement was made that the school would become a secondary modern school called Ashlyns,[16] and gradually the boarders and the day pupils began to merge into a single school, with the younger Coram children being sent to live with foster parents.

From 1952 to 1954 the minutes of the governors' policy committee show deeply divided views as to what to do with the remaining children for whom they were responsible. The headmaster Mr Gilbertson recommended keeping the older children in a boarding house as he felt the stigma would be greater if they were to return to their foster parents than if they stayed at the school. He argued that boarding school was character forming and good for the children, with good food, healthy surroundings, good routine, the swimming pool, music, etc.

Miss Ashworth, recently appointed as the charity's first children's officer in response to the 1948 Children Act, was a key figure in the transformation of Coram from the residential institution that it had been for so long to the fostering agency it was to become for the next twenty years. She recommended that children should, wherever possible, be brought up in foster homes even if that meant leaving the school, or if this was not possible then in a small house for a mixed family group. Her views were confirmed by a letter from the Home Office in 1954 which said that 'while any change of school may have disadvantages, it is not considered that these would outweigh the benefits to the children if they were given the opportunity to become established in foster homes in which they could continue to live after leaving school and entering employment.' In April 1954 the Secretary wrote to foster parents to say that after consulting with the Children's Department of the Home Office, the governors had decided, with regret, to close the boarding side of the school. The children were to remain in foster homes and go to local schools.

With the departure of the last children, Handel's organ was moved to St Andrews Church in Holborn, though it had to be virtually rebuilt. Thomas Coram's body was removed from the chapel and interred in St Andrews in 1960.

In 1957 the governors published their first annual report for eleven years, referring to the metamorphosis that had occurred since the last report. Their current policy was:

> … to lay great emphasis on the home atmosphere for the children – primarily, of course, by restoration to the mother, and secondly by adoption and thirdly (and principally) by the choice of suitable foster parents. In furtherance of the first of these objects a lot of time is being devoted to so-called 'case work' with the mother with a view to rehabilitation – and this is beginning to be remarkably successful. In fact, nearly 50 per cent of our children are now either restored to their mothers or adopted – a most gratifying state of affairs.

The report also refers to a generous gift from Mrs Plant, a governor and the daughter and granddaughter of former treasurers – Sir Roger Gregory and George Gregory MP – with which the governors decided to build Gregory House on the Coram Campus, a building still used by Coram Family today. Mrs Plant herself is reported as saying at the OCA Charter Day dinner:

> the story concerning the school was a very sad one, but it was necessary for us to remember that the march

of the welfare state had greatly influenced the present position. It was the intention of the governors to review the activities of the Foundation and fill in the gaps in the present welfare structure, which, she said, would be what Captain Coram would have wished in changing circumstances.[17]

Admissions were reduced to about twenty-five babies a year, but in 1957 there were still 500 children in the care of the Thomas Coram Foundation. Between 1950 and 1980 the Thomas Coram Foundation was largely a foster care agency, and since 1976 Coram has provided former pupils with similar information as is now available to adopted people – their birth certificate and also a history of their parental background, prepared from the mother's confidential papers by an experienced social worker. This work is described more fully in Chapter VIII.

And so an era slowly came to an end. With the benefit of hindsight, our current knowledge about the emotional needs of children, and the importance of maintaining close relationships between parents and children wherever possible, it is easy to be critical of the governors of the Foundling Hospital for their response to the needs of the children they took into their care and the time they took to change their views. But even during the early part of the twentieth century, the stigma of illegitimacy remained, and before the establishment of the welfare state after the end of the Second World War, young mothers who were given no support from their child's father struggled to survive. Finally pressures from both within and without the organisation forced change and, from being the first children's residential home, the Foundling Hospital became one of the first to give all of its children the benefit of family life, as the Thomas Coram Foundation for Children in 1955. Since its inception in 1739 it had cared for 25,000 children, the vast majority for the whole of their childhood, from a few days old until they reached the age of twenty-one.

WHO AM I? WHERE DID I COME FROM? FORMER PUPILS LOOK BACK ON THEIR CHILDHOOD EXPERIENCES

The children in the care of the Foundling Hospital lived in the Foundling Hospital in Bloomsbury at the beginning of the century (until 1926), then at Redhill (1926–1935) and then at Berkhamsted (1935–1955). In this chapter we hear from former pupils who experienced life in all of these settings, using material from interviews and some published reports and articles.

In order to provide a broad summary of life in the Foundling Hospital, we start with extended quotations from Harold Tarrant, born in 1911 and the only former pupil to be made a governor of the Foundling Hospital.[1] His account is similar to others of this period[2] and these will be drawn on throughout the chapter:

> I am Harold Tarrant, I was admitted to the Foundling Hospital in February 1912.

On the day I came up to the Foundling Hospital there were two other boys. We would have been taken into the school infirmary and checked. Then we went into the chapel and were baptised and I became Harold Tarrant. My birth name Noel Patrick Brew disappeared forever.

On that day three foster mothers came up from Kent and I went down to Hadlow where I was fostered by a Mr and Mrs Palmer, who had a lovely old farm, a lovely farm house, there was a large barn; stables, with a couple of big farm horses; another one for the pony that pulled the trap, there were pig sties, chicken houses and fields.

Mrs Palmer was a lovely cook and it was an absolutely idyllic life for a young child. One of my happiest memories was going with my foster father, I called him dad of course, not knowing any better, with one of the horses down to Hadlow – to the blacksmith. Life was absolutely carefree and I have only one sad memory that was, one day I fell carrying a glass which broke and I badly cut my left wrist. Mum washed it and dad harnessed up the pony and trap and I was rushed down to Dr. Lawrence in the village. He cleaned it up and stitched it and I still have the scars.

There were three of us there at different times. When I first went to the foster home, Emily R was there – she left after about two years, I never understood why. Shortly after Alfred E joined – I never knew why.

I remember Doctor Mitchell coming to the farm-house vaccinating me and giving me a thorough examination, it had no significance with me. About two months later Mrs Palmer took me across the road to stand outside the public house where the horse bus stopped. When it came in a lady stepped out with a list 'Tarrant?' … 'present?' I joined the bus and, there were several stops, before we came to Tonbridge Station. Then a number of foster mothers with children boarded the train – we thought this was quite an adventure.

When we arrived in London we were met by a Mr and Mrs Brunz taken to a waiting horse bus and driven through what seemed to us very busy streets, coming up from the country and then we stopped at some big iron gates and a little man who we later got to know as Mr Moffit the gate porter unlocked and opened up these vast gates and we drove through and stopped in front of the piazza which was in front of the chapel. As we alighted our names were again called and we stood with our foster mothers wondering what was going to happen next. Then, two by two names were called – two nurses took boys away struggling and crying and they disappeared we knew not where. This went on and I happened to be among the last two. I remember I held on like mad but it was useless. We went along the piazza through a dark passage and through grounds which I came to know as infirmary. Then we went up some up some iron steps at the side of a building which was House 40. As we entered there was pandemonium. I was quickly undressed and bathed and then inspected by Dr. Swift the school doctor. Then dressed in uniform – short trousers, a purply sort of colour. There was lots of crying.

That night when we went to bed we were told to kneel by our beds and say our prayers. There was no goodnight hug or kiss and in the morning our dreams were not realised as we were still there.

The following day, Mr Clap the barber came along – cut our hair and then cut it very close to the scalp with his clippers. We now looked like institutional children. We lost our personality.

Life at House 40 was very dull. The food after my foster mother's cooking was awful. I've never forgotten the boiled rice served in lumps. But, we got accustomed to it. Our foster mothers were not allowed to visit us during all this time. Then came the day when we were transferred to the infants' school. This was a big airy room. At one end there were tiers of wooden seats.

Miss Bateman was the head teacher, white hair, quite kindly but a strict individual. Assisted by Miss Ducy and Miss Blane – I've never forgotten any of them. Then came the day when Miss Bateman called out a number of names and said 'you're going to the big boys' school and you're going to the big girls' school'. We waited then were separated. We didn't realise we would probably never speak to those girls again. It was complete segregation. Even foster brothers and foster sisters and those who had been fostered together.

When we arrived at the boys' school, our infant school uniform was taken and we were dressed in the boy's uniform which consisted of long trousers which we looked forward to, a bright red waist coat with red buttons, a jacket also with buttons, except for a button at the top – no pockets. Quite smart, but not exactly comfortable.

There were four wards – that night we went into the fourth ward. Wards for the two youngest boys had a room at the end where there was a nurse. In the fourth ward it was nurse Gosling, of course we called her 'Goosie'. She was quite a kindly soul. The wards had bare boards. At one end there was a zinc sheet and a pan. In the rest, nothing.

In the morning we would be called to wash and then go down to the basement to the boot room. There were lockers for each boy where you had to put your boots – your Sunday boots, your day boots and your plimsolls during the day. We would queue up for the boot brushes but because the basement was rarely visited by a master it was a place where there was a lot of bullying. I remember, the younger boys would be lining up and a boy would run along with a wet towel and hit us all. They would also say 'come on you two fight'. Those of us who had older foster brothers were very fortunate because they were our protectors. Alfred Foxcroft looked after me and protected me from any bullying. Of course we made other friends, some of whom were our friends throughout our school days. Our 'mates' we used to call them.

Each morning we lined up in the common room for classes. Boys who were standing on the platform were caned and classes were marched off one by one. The teacher for the lowest class was a Miss Stevenson. A very kindly lady – it doesn't sound a lot now but I recall that on each boy's birthday she would get the class to stand up and sing 'Happy Birthday' and she would give the boy a sweet. It was the only occasion when somebody got a sweet and it wasn't from their foster mothers.

In addition to our lessons we fortunately had a good school library from which we were able to borrow books one a week but of course we could exchange. But our greatest prize of a book was Pears Encyclopaedia – this was full of items about sport, history and general knowledge.

Each morning we would be sent out into the playground no matter how cold – no hats – no gloves – and to run round and keep warm. We didn't think much of it at the time but it was probably very good for us. There were arches along side the playground where we could go when it was raining. There was very little sports equipment, in fact the boys used to make 'rag balls'. Mr Holgate was the headmaster, we called him 'digger' – very rude really. But we thought he must have had piles! He was a brute of a man. I've never forgiven him, even now, for the heavy punishment he used to give some of the boys, particularly those who wet their beds. He knew, we knew, they couldn't help it but he flogged them unmercifully.

There were occasions when outsiders came and inspected us. I remember the Duke of Connaught, who was a vice president I think, and there was an occasion when, following the parade of the governors and the Duke of Connaught – one boy wrote about this – after the lunch one of the boys ate the duke's remains!

We lived a very enclosed life, never allowed to go out. We were never allowed to approach nearer than about twelve feet from the gates. Presumably in case somebody wanted to talk to us. The only occasions we went out was going to various theatres.

We were always cared for in the school infirmary. We made occasional visits for a dose of rhubarb and soda. There had been an occasion in 1922 when measles was widespread so much so that one of the boy's wards had to be used as an infirmary ward. I was one of those with measles which was followed by discharging ears, and then I had a painful swollen shoulder. On December 23rd 1922 in the afternoon Dr. Furley came back for his second visit with a white haired gentleman who examined me and looked at my papers. Half an hour later I was in a taxi to St. Bartholomew's hospital. I was taken straight up to a ward and that evening I had an operation on my left shoulder because of an abscess. When I awoke I was as sick as a dog because at that time one had 'ether' and I noticed the ward was gaily decorated – a thing I was not accustomed to. On Christmas morning when I awoke Nurse Salter tended to me, sat me up in bed and started to open a parcel. I remember I cried and cried. She said 'what's the matter?' 'what's the matter?' I never understood at the time but it was the first time since I left my foster home that I had personal care, and I was in any case, very weak. I stayed in St. Bartholomew's for a month, then I was sent to a convalescent home for another month which perhaps explains why years later I was walking out with Kathy, who I eventually married, in Redhill and we saw one of the teachers coming along – it was too late to cross the road … 'poor boy poor boy, always ill! always ill!' – it wasn't really true I was always spectacularly ill! And significantly when my present doctor first saw my wound on my arm, because I had a further operation a week later, and asked me what it was, he said 'you're lucky to be alive'. He said an abscess is difficult to treat even now but in those days without antibiotics you were very, very lucky.

Each year we spent our six week summer holiday at camp under canvas. We exchanged our uniforms for khaki shirts and shorts, long woollen socks and Baden Powell hats. There was great excitement for weeks ahead. I remember camps at Henley-On-Thames, Brocken Green, Worthing, Bracknell, Bognor and my favourite, in 1925 and 1926 at Aldridges' Farm at Whitchurch near Pangbourne.

There the tents were pitched within site but not within the smell of the farm yard. Mr Aldridge was very kindly disposed towards us and he allowed small groups to wander around the farm yard and see the animals. Heaven to a boy like me, with my happy memories of my foster parent's home.

In our first camp at Aldridges' farm we boys were playing on a lovely sunny day, out came one of the masters and told us to clear off. I said quite audibly 'we won't be allowed in the camp soon' He said 'you go and stand next to Mr Holgate's tent'. I knew what that meant. Several other boys were standing there. We missed our tea and I was getting quite annoyed. Then we were sent for by one of the masters. Each one in turn was asked why he was standing there and received a caning. When I was asked I said we were told to clear off when we were playing in bounds and I said so, he told me touch my toes, I stood defiant – he hit me with the cane – we grappled, fell on the floor, he knelt on my arms, he said 'you'll touch your toes'. I said 'we were in bounds sir, I will not!'. We stood up, he said, 'you go and stand by Mr Holgate's tent again, he'll know what to do with you'. I stood there lonely waiting for him to come, the boys went to bed and I was still there, then I think the master on duty had got somebody to wait for Mr Holgate's return and he came into his tent, I listened hard but couldn't hear what they were saying. Then Mr Brunz came over (he was a general labourer on the site) and he disappeared. When he came back Mr Holgate came out of the tent and said 'Tarrant I won't have insubordination – you're not fit to be with the other boys for the rest of the camp you will be on your own in a separate tent working the cook house'. I followed Mr Brunz to a lovely staff tent, carpet on the floor, spring mattress, wash basin, nice chair, I thought this is good! In the morning I went to the cook house – the cook said 'what would you like for breakfast son?', I thought life was marvellous!

My longest period at camp was in 1926. We had left the Foundling Hospital in London for good and the school in Redhill was not yet ready. We had classes but life was still very good. We went by train to Redhill. The band had their instruments on board, we all formed up outside the station, I was at that time drum major. We awaited for Mr Holgate to say quick march and off we went. Unfortunately Mr Own the band master had disappeared from sight. Well we left the site, I wasn't sure where to turn left or right, and then I saw him. Fortunately had we gone the wrong way we would have gone up a steep hill and I've often wondered how on earth we would have managed from then on! The Redhill school was in the country, a bit more comfortable than the London school and I remained there until December.

We were all lined up for classes, Mr Holgate went along the row 'Tarrant, Ashurst, Brown, Barsfield, Ablet, Haverfield, Monotype', who on earth was Monotype we thought? But we had learnt better than to ask Mr Holgate any questions. We waited until we got up in class and asked Mr Morley, 'Who's Monotype Sir?', he said 'he's not a person, that's where you're going to be engineering apprentices'. That was not the first job I had been offered.

We used to take our showers in a shower room in the basement and one day Mr Holgate was on duty and he shouted up and we all hurried up as the last one probably got a cane on his bottom and I heard 'Tarrant!' and I thought 'good heavens what have I done now?!'. I went smartly to him and stood to attention 'sir?', 'Canada' he said. 'I'm only 13 sir' I said, he said 'dismissed'. That was the first job I lost.

Most of the boys who were fit to pass the army test were enlisted as band boys. This was very appropriate. We had been brought up like little militarists – we'd been members of an army style band and a boy going into the army was no further cost to the hospital. They would be placed on a train and told where to get off. I remember the story of three boys told to get off at Tidworth. When they got out at the station they saw a soldier and said 'excuse me sir, where's Tidworth Barracks?' he looked them up and down and said 'are you from a concert party?!' and they said 'no sir, this is our uniform'.

We who were apprentices had to be fully kitted out in civilian clothes. We earned so little the hospital had to pay for our lodgings. The day we left was December 8th, 1926. We left in taxis and went into lodgings in Redhill.

I think most of us looked forward to leaving school. It was a harsh regime, particularly through the Headmaster who was a brute of a man. We led a very disciplined existence and one could not help reflecting back on one's early years in a lovely foster home.

Sadly my foster mother died whilst I was still at school. All our correspondence was opened before being passed to us, no comment was made in the letter which said my mother had died and I was just left to sit and cry on my own.

I realise that my mother had had little alternative but to place me in the care of the Foundling Hospital, I was well cared for – led a very disciplined life, and looked forward to leaving.

I think it probably set me up well in life, my spartan up bringing has perhaps accounted for my 92 years and also one had many friends. Life long friends.

It is not a life I would have wished upon anybody else.

There are many themes within Harold Tarrant's account that run through other interviews and written accounts. In almost all of these accounts former pupils look back on their time in the country with their foster parents (who they thought were their real parents) as idyllic, and there are a number of references to foster mothers in particular as the unsung heroes of the Foundling Hospital. Despite the levels of poverty in the country homesteads, the children felt they were loved and revelled in the freedom they were given. A study of twenty-five former pupils found that most of the foster fathers were farm labourers, gardeners or working in various manual trades. Foster mothers were described as being home orientated, absorbed in the domestic responsibilities of cooking, cleaning and childcare.[3] The children were often brought up alongside the biological children and sometimes with other foster children. They describe feeling cared for and enjoying the freedom to play in orchards and fields:

> No child … was ever heard to complain about the treatment they received at the hands of their foster parents. Some were so happy that they later took for themselves the family names of their foster parents … to underline their gratitude … This was indeed a happy time, and many nostalgic memories remain. Gram's cooking, and how she managed such a wide variety of dishes on the simply tiny coal fired cooking range … the multiplicity of Gram's pies, all baked in an oven whose temperature was dependant on the state of the adjacent fire. There was home made jam from the gooseberries in the back garden … wild

rabbits would be left on the doorstep by friendly farm workers … money was meagre, Gram managed everything on her tiny widows pension together with the money paid by the Foundling Hospital for my upkeep. There was always enough and more, and the house full of warmth, kindness, love and mirth was a wonderful home.[4]

Charles Nalden, who wrote an autobiography of his life in the Foundling Hospital, as an army bandsman, and as a musician in New Zealand, also describes going from being an unwanted baby to a very much wanted foster child. He paints a very vivid picture of the small house and garden in Chertsey, with a front parlour that was only used on special occasions, bath night in the galvanised iron tub in the kitchen, the country walks, the brass bands and fairs and circuses, and saving up for Christmas. But unlike some of his contemporaries, he was constantly reminded of his eventual return to the 'Fondling 'orsepiddle'.[5]

There were of course some whose experience was less happy, as for this woman whose first foster mother became ill and who was subsequently placed with one who emotionally and physically abused her:

Just how I survived it, I don't know. So coming to school was a certain safety. I knew she wasn't going to school I knew she was going home and I would not be beaten … she used to shut me in the chicken run at night. She tried every which way to kill me.

(Helen aged sixty)[6]

But the overall impression was of "blossoming" and of a sense of belonging'.[7] It is of course possible that, in contrast to the years that followed, this period became over-idealised, but the attachments that the children formed to their foster parents were very real and were important in helping them to develop the resilience that they required to cope with the guilt and sense of rejection that would stay with them for the rest of their lives.

If the years in their foster families provided them with a good second start in life, the shock when the doors of the Foundling Hospital clanged shut behind them and they became part of the institution are palpable in all the former pupils' accounts, as illustrated by Harold Tarrant and by May, aged seventy-two at the time of this interview, who went to Redhill:

> And the next memory was getting to Redhill and this very big building and having all our hair shaved off …
> I remember Bill [foster parents' biological son] saying to me 'don't cry'. I had this in my mind. 'Don't cry'. I can remember this big stone room that had iron beds and there were two bed-heads put together like that. And there was a little boy in the other bed and he was crying all the time 'I want my mummy'. And I remember putting my hands through and holding his hand and thinking I must not cry. I had promised Bill I wouldn't cry.[8]

The details of daily life have been summarised by Harold Tarrant. The daily routines, the parades and the bands, the separation of the boys from the girls after the infant

stage, all of this had changed little from Dickens time
and are described by Nalden as 'a monotonous day to
day, month to month, year to year style of living'.[9] The
uniformity of dress and routine, and the isolation from
the outside world, all reduced the children's sense of
personal identity. The absence of information or expla-
nation did not help:

> ... all the time at the back of your mind, you were
> thinking 'What's happened to me? Where did I come
> from? Where am I going?, you know. And this is the
> traumatic part really about it all. You feel that you're in
> a situation where you've foster people and they've left
> you. Nobody tells you why it happened, you know?
> ... So when I went to bed and you were on your
> own, you'd think 'what have I done?' and begin to feel
> guilty that you'd done something to cause it ...
>
> (Jack, aged seventy-nine)[10]

This lack of information is echoed by two former
pupils who were interviewed by Kate Adie for her book
Nobody's Child, about foundlings. Lydia Wingate had no
idea why she was at Berkhamsted, nor why she was called
what she was:

> Obviously we knew we were different, and we didn't
> have a family. We didn't talk about ourselves much, just
> sometimes asked each other if 'Mum' [foster mother]
> was coming up on 'Mums' day' [the day for visits from
> foster mothers]. We weren't told anything, except a
> governor – who'd found me being naughty – once

told me we were there to 'serve the public'. No one ever sat us down and told us why we hadn't got real mummies and daddies.

John Caldicott thinks that the reason that they accepted this 'life of service' was:

> because there was something shameful. ... I can never remember anyone saying to me 'You were born out of wedlock' But it was made very, very clear that our mothers had done something wrong, and that we were also to blame. We were guilty and we felt guilty, and the interesting thing is that guilt follows you through life – it doesn't disappear.[11]

The children were also very isolated from other children and from everyday life. In London the children seldom went out beyond the gates, apart from the occasional visit to the circus or the theatre. But in Berkhamsted there were few such visits, and it was not even possible to watch the world go by as the school was some way from the centre of the town. At one point the children were commanded to parade around the grounds, as the local people were beginning to think that they did not exist.

Everything was regulated, and the children were isolated from any interface with the outside world. Over 400 children were washed, dressed, fed, exercised, and given a basic education to a strict daily routine:

> You couldn't say anything. You sort of went along with everything. And then, like a lot of sheep you're herded

here. Sit down. You're having a meal. Up you get, and
so on. Just from one place to the other ... And you
don't realise anything. You just go along, there's no
alternative. And I think I just – you sort of clam up ...
I was free before ... and I was finding I could think for
myself and ... then you went to the school and you
lost that ... so you clammed up.

(Patricia aged seventy)[12]

Charles Nalden cites the total segregation of boys and
girls as deriving from a 'fear of bastards begetting bastards.' On the rare occasions when the boys and girls did
meet, it is deeply etched on the writer's memory – as for
example one incident in 1946 when the doors dividing
the dining room in half were drawn back at tea time and
twins – a boy and a girl – met for the first time in years
over a birthday cake and candles. As Tom Erskine says,
'They just looked at each other with their heads cocked
at identical but opposite angles, and grinned identical
grins. What passed between them as they sat together
for the very first time on their birthday I will never
know.'[13] John Caldicott describes this event, and the subsequent mixing of girls and boys in classes, as 'perhaps the
most significant change to the lives of the children ...
The result was "electric" to be able to observe the "other
side"'[14] This was also the time when the school uniform
was abolished.

The education improved during the twentieth century
and particularly after the 1944 Education Act and the
return from the war of some better qualified teachers.
In some areas, for example music, gym and swimming,

many former pupils felt they were way ahead of pupils in other schools. For example, when talking about the arrival of local children in the school in the 1950s one former pupil said 'We were better runners, better swimmers, we were fitter, better fed, better clothed, all very healthy and some of the town kids were quite poor … I swam like a fish, That was fun.'[15] And this interview with a former pupil took place in the presence of her husband and daughter:

June: Swimming. We had our own swimming baths, and we used to play netball, cricket. They were very good … And they taught us to swim.

Daughter: … Dad's never learned to swim, has he. If you compared my mum's years as a child to my dad, my mum had far more than he did.

June: Because our parents …

Husband: She did far more things than I ever done. I never went to no circus.

Daughter: And he was an only child as well.

Husband: Yes. And all the opportunity I suppose of being on the outside Just mum and dad. But they [pointing to his wife] were doing well, I'll tell you. You had to go out with the dog and catch a rabbit in my time.

(Interview with June, aged eighty-three)[16]

One or two of the brighter girls started going to Camden School each year, and went on to university, as is cited in this letter to *The Times,* which also pays tribute to the governors for their continuing support and aftercare for their pupils:

My mother was admitted to The Foundling Hospital in central London in January 1915 at the age of nine weeks and grew up in its care. Most girls were placed in service when they reached school-leaving age but in the 1920s, realising they had some academically bright girls, Coram's rented a house in Hampstead and used it as a home for a dozen girls, my mother among them, who were enrolled at the prestigious (and fee paying) Camden High School for Girls. My mother went on to London University, with full financial support from Coram's throughout.

After graduating in 1936 she wanted a secretarial qualification too, and Coram's again paid for the best, sending her to the top-flight St James Secretarial College in Belgravia (the only place the governors had heard of, it was rumoured, as their debutante daughters went there).

Although it could not compensate for the emotional deprivation she had suffered as a child, this unstintingly generous education stood my mother in excellent stead in her career, thanks to the far sightedness of that unique institution, The Foundling Hospital, now Coram Family.[17]

The health care was generally considered good, particularly the care in the infirmary where Nalden describes the firm discipline and good care provided by Sister Cleeve, 'the school's most commanding personality'. Harold Tarrant wasn't the only one to find that a stay in hospital brought its own rewards, as this description of a hospital stay when twenty girls developed measles in 1920 illustrates:

It was a miserable and disappointing Christmas …
No pantomimes, Christmas tree parties and above all
no Bertram Mills Circus which was a regular treat
each year … Some of the children also developed
scarlet fever and were sent to St Ann's Hospital for
Infectious Diseases in Totttenham, and were then
quarantined because a boy there developed smallpox.
I have happy memories of getting half an orange or
an apple with a sweet each day – we never had anything like that in school … We were allowed to stroll
around the grounds under supervision and we felt as
free as birds on the wing (so different from our rigid
routine at school).[18]

The writer also remembers food parcels from generous foster parents, and forbidden picnics – and stayed
in hospital until the end of August, in time for the
summer camp.

Several former pupils testify to the fact that there was
no sexual abuse in the Foundling Hospital, although of
course it is not possible to know if this was the experience of all pupils. Some of the staff, however, are still
remembered for their harsh discipline, particularly the
headmaster Mr Holgate who retired in 1943 after forty
years at the Hospital. 'Mr Holgate was hated by the boys
for his brutality, in particular those unfortunate enough
to wet the bed. He ran the boys side of the school with an
iron fist and his crooked cane.'[19] There was also a degree
of bullying (as often as not by the senior pupils as much
as by the staff), particularly during the war years when
morale was low and discipline lax. Some of this probably

started as fun and games, as for example the tradition of chariot races which several former pupils describe:

> … One of the games I remember we played very often was chariots. Where they would have four boys, two standing up, and two bending over holding onto the two boys, and then the elder boys would use this as a chariot and race up and down the dormitories, crashing into each other without very much concern for the young children who were carrying them … very similar to other boarding schools of the time.[20]

What was missing was the emotional support, which often led to low self-esteem and a difficulty in forming relationships in later life. One former pupil describes bath nights as a small child:

> Kids are incredibly aware, they see everything. I saw the big arms of the nurses, their fleshy arms, and the way they were doing this job, bathing us. They didn't count us as people … I remember nurse S and she would raise her arms to a kid who was crying, and she threatened … They weren't arms to protect us.[21]

Another woman describes not being able to take her 'cuddly' panda to bed with her, but having to put it on the floor:

> The absence of 'good enough' parental figures and such restrictions contributed to making me unhappy. I was afraid of doing anything wrong, cried a great

deal, and was often ill. This is not to deny some happy times, but such moments were fraught with fear lest they be snatched away too.[22]

In the Hospital itself many former pupils speak of the regime leading to a lack of close friendships:

> One of the interesting things about being a border in the Foundling Hospital was that you didn't really make close friends. We used to have gangs but nobody became your personal friend and it was not encouraged. You were expected simply to live with each other impersonally and I think it goes back to how we were expected to view life in general. In the early days before the changes we were clearly made to understand that we were very lucky to be at the Foundling Hospital. That we were second class citizens in so much as we had been born out of wedlock and that our mothers had been given a special chance to repair her life without us. We never really understood what this was all about. We would spend hours dreaming that our mothers were queens and princesses and hopefully one day they would come and reclaim us, but of course they never did.[23]

Leaving the school led to difficulties in forming relationships, particularly with the opposite sex. Many former pupils speak of having very low self-esteem and an inferiority complex, which some felt 'stopped us becoming leaders – we always expected to be told what to do'. Others speak of the how little they knew about the facts of life. In the early part of the century it was a punishable offence among the girls to share information about menstruation or reproduction, and even in the 1940s for example, one former pupil said: 'no-one had told us anything about sex or boys. The very first time a boy kissed me – and it wasn't even a passionate kiss, I remember in the toilet saying "Please God don't let me be pregnant."'[24] Then there were also the practical difficulties for children who had never bought a bus ticket, used money, turned a light switch on gone to the pictures, made a cup of tea, or mixed socially with other children.

There were also the challenges of establishing a good family life, when there was no experience to draw on – or even understanding what family life was. One former pupil said 'I could never understand why a married woman had a mother; I could never understand why those who weren't married had the same name as their parents.'[25] And how did you get to know about how children should be brought up? Another woman, now in her nineties, said 'We had a very strict upbringing, and I was very hard on my own children, until I discovered there were lots of grey patches in life for which one had to make allowances.'[26] Much depended on the warmth and understanding of a supportive wife or husband:

> I think the biggest effect is probably family, because you don't know how to live with a family; you don't know how to live with a wife and you don't know how to bring up children … I think there is regret in two areas … my lost childhood and theirs, because I was never really able to be a father in the

same way I see fathers today. But I'm very successful
with my grandchildren. Totally different and a totally
different relationship.[27]

The fact that so many former pupils have lived reasonably happy and successful lives, marrying and bringing up
their own children, suggests that they developed an inner
resilience despite the guilt and shame of being illegitimate
and the harshness of the regime. In part, as was suggested
earlier, this can be attributed to the warmth and nurtur-
ing relationships that most former pupils enjoyed with
their foster parents in the crucial first five years of life.
But there were other experiences and individuals who
brought light, hope and enjoyment to the children – particularly key members of staff, the annual summer camps,
the music that was such a central part of institutional life,
and outings and special happenings.

Although the Foundling Hospital had its share of harsh
disciplinarians and poorly trained staff, some stand out
from the interviews and accounts as bringing a human
touch to a uniform institution. For Hannah Brown it
was the seamstress who took her on as a maid and the
organist who called the girls his darlings. For generations of musicians it was the bandmaster Mr Owen or
one of his successors. Mr Gray, who married the matron,
had former pupils visit the couple after they had left
school, and were remembered by many; as was Mr Tidey,
the bread man and later caretaker of the Child Welfare
building in London, who always had a kind word for the
children and also kept in touch with many of them after
they had left school. And in the earlier days of the century

the chaplain Revd Stork who took the boys for games
and was described by Harold Tarrant as 'one of nature's
gentlemen', kept in touch with many former pupils and
encouraged the children to 'AIM HIGH, AIM HIGH!
He who aims at the noonday sun, though he will never
reach his goal, yet he will get further than he who aims
but at a bush.'[28]

Music was the highlight of many children's lives, and
for some it provided a passport into the outside world as
they went on to careers in music, or playing in orchestras
and bands for enjoyment. Charles Nalden, for example, went on to become professor of music at Auckland
University in New Zealand after a distinguished career as
an army bandmaster. Others also had much to be thank-
ful for: 'I think the education we received at the Thomas
Coram School was very good, I was particularly grateful
for the grounding in music we received – something I
have followed up and enjoyed throughout my life.'[29] And:

> Mr Owen's big foot beating time on my little one in
> the Band room, and the knock on my head from his
> grey stubble forehead when I got it right on my Bb
> clarinet. Little did I realise that beautiful man had pro-
> vided me (and I'm sure a lot of others) with five years
> of pure heaven in a jazz band in Weybridge.[30]

For some it brightened up a drab week and provided a
temporary escape into a different world:

> Music did play a major role and Sundays were the best
> day. I remember the peace and serenity of the chapel,

and the organ and choir. It wasn't until I was 14 or
15 that I ever admitted something was beautiful. I joined
the choir, and revelled in that. It was another world,
away from the Foundling Hospital.[31]

And for others it made a profound difference as they
tried to develop a sense of who they were:

> From the age of 12 I have always loved classical music,
> a love that started in the infirmary where I was recov-
> ering from an asthma attack. I remember to this day
> suddenly hearing Tchaikovsky's "serenade for strings"
> over the tannoy. A new world opened up and I devel-
> oped what subsequently became a passion for music
> and which later extended to all the arts. Looking back,
> I see this as a pivotal moment in my life, a recognition
> that there would always be a never ending supply of
> good things … At age 24 I had another moment of rev-
> elation, when I realised that music touched the centre
> of my life and everything would always be all right.[32]

There were also special events, particularly at Christmas,
though accounts of such events vary with some former
pupils remembering the excitement of the Christmas
tree and the lights and the special food, and others the
disappointment at the lack of presents. When the children were still in London, there were visits to Bertram
Mills circus, and to the theatre, but this was more difficult
from Redhill and Berkhamsted.

Once foster mothers were allowed to visit this too
became a highlight, at least for those children whose

mothers were able to come. For those who had none, it
was yet another rejection:

> Our mothers used to come and see us once in three
> months, and we all used to look forward to that day and
> pity anybody who didn't have anybody to see them,
> although it wasn't a regular occurrence as most people
> had somebody to see them. It unsettled us for a day or
> two afterwards, but we soon settled down again to our
> old routine.[33]

Some former pupils remember receiving Christmas and
birthday presents that they later discovered were from
their birth family:

> My mother and grandmother sent lots of letters
> to the school, asking them to give me a toy for my
> birthday or let them know how I was. They sent
> presents regularly, but I didn't get them, or if I did
> I was never told who they were from. If I'd known
> they were from my mother it would have meant
> something different.[34]

But perhaps the event which caused the greatest excitement and which was looked forward to with the most
anticipation (or 'glished' in the pupils' special language)
was the annual summer camp (see illustrations 28–35).
The accounts of holidays under canvas have the same
feel about them as do the accounts of the years living
with foster parents – relaxation in the country, the fun
and the freedom of being able to spend the small sums

of money that had been saved up during the year; of wearing lighter weight clothes; of playing in the woods and picking wild flowers; and walking behind the band as the children marched from the station to the camp site.

The camps and the outings were suspended during the years of the Second World War, and the children who were at Berkamstead during this period felt that they missed out on the few really enjoyable aspects of school life.

Before leaving these accounts, we should note that some former pupils looked back with nostalgia and affection, seemingly untainted by the traumatic memories of their colleagues. Mary Bentley is by no means the only person to speak in these tones:

> I settled down and I loved school, Absolutely loved it … We were taught games, and a love of the classic books. Music was another thing we were taught to love, right from early childhood … Education was basic but very good … I remember very well the day we moved to Berkhamsted, it was a beautiful day and I remember getting into the new corridors and everybody shouting because of the echo of the new building … We did enjoy our time there and I must say I was very happy – I loved school and was sad when the day came for me to leave. We made many friends, many of whom we keep in touch with today.[35]

It is beyond the scope of this book to follow the accounts of the former pupils into their later lives, as they sought employment and began to create their own families, and sometimes to search out their families of origin, although some of this is covered in Chapter eight. But perhaps the last word should go to this woman writing in *Coram News*:

> The strict regime we all endured has made me a fighter and a survivor . The words Foundling Hospital brought further problems as I went to seek my fortune. It caused hands to be raised in absolute horror, by the Establishment, financial institutions in the City, solicitors and accountants. One day it dawned on me, another two words would receive a different reaction – 'boarding school.' It has never ceased to amaze me, why these two words assume you are one of them. From that day on I was in.[36]

These accounts provide a vivid insight into how it felt to be a child growing up in the Foundling Hospital. Although the regime was harsh, as indeed were many public schools at the time, it was the stigma and the rejection that marked these children out. As John Caldicott, now Secretary of the Old Coram Association says:

> I spent many years as a little boy in a state of almost permanent terror, not necessarily because of the regime at the hospital, but because of the rejection I had suffered and because I really never knew what was going to happen to me next. Looking back, it was all about rejection … With hindsight I'm very grateful to the Foundling Hospital for all it did for me … But we didn't feel lucky when we were there.[37]

Val Molloy, an experienced social worker with Coram Family, who works with former pupils in supporting them to find their birth families, puts this into perspective:

> It is not my belief that the care offered by the Foundling Hospital was deliberately designed to be cruel or damaging, or to heap further adversity onto the lives of children already born into difficult circumstances. The Foundling Hospital had started as a fundamentally benevolent institution and in many practical respects (education, nutrition, medical care) offered above average care when compared with that received by many work-class children of the time. What was lacking was lacking throughout all social care institutions at the time, simply because the body of theory and research that has led to our present day understanding of child development had not yet taken shape. Explanations of attachment and loss and theoretical concepts such as 'identity' had not yet been established and generally accepted.[38]

VIII

FROM THOMAS CORAM FOUNDATION FOR CHILDREN TO CORAM FAMILY: 1955–2005

It is a sunny afternoon in June 2005 and the Coram Community Campus is alive with the sound of music. Some 200 small children and their parents and nursery staff are taking part in the annual Coram music day in the courtyard outside Coram's headquarters and the children's centre building at the northern end of the old Foundling Hospital site. Parents join in the singing and dancing rhymes with their babies in their arms, whilst Margaretta, who runs the very popular music sessions in the Parents Centre, leads the group on her accordion. The infants and toddlers perform songs using drums, tambourines and cymbals, followed by the three and four year-olds singing and acting some of the songs they have learnt during the term. With the help of Tiffany, the music therapist, some of the children who find communicating through language very difficult are happy to take part with the rest of the group, and the children who attend groups run by KIDS, the special needs charity based on the campus, also join in the fun. Next on, after a break for juice and fruit, a steel band from the local primary school plays. The excitement is mounting.

Upstairs in the Coram adoption offices the staff are planning the adoption picnic which will take place at the weekend in Collingham Gardens, the green 'oasis' adjoining the campus. This grassy area, once a graveyard back in the seventeenth century, is a haven of peace and tranquillity in the centre of London, and the perfect spot for a weekend celebration. About fifty families are expected, with the children they have adopted through Coram, and they are all looking forward to this annual treat – as are the Coram staff who get great satisfaction from seeing how well the children are developing in their adoptive families.

Early in September, Collingham Gardens will also be the venue for further celebrations and a barbecue – this time the celebration of achievement ceremony for about 100 young people who have been part of Coram's leaving care service. Some will, for the first time, have passed exams ranging from basic numeracy and literacy through to computer skills and art and crafts; others will have worked closely with their mentors to achieve personal goals related to their education, their behaviour, or their social skills; others will have written poetry or music, or helped friends and colleagues.

England in the early years of the twenty-first century is a very different place from the post-war Britain of the 1950s, and Coram has had to adapt its work with children and families to respond to the changes in their lives. Writing at the turn of the century, Gillian Pugh pointed to some of the key demographic and environmental

factors that are affecting families. The range and diversity
of families living in Britain would have been inconceiv-
able 100 or even 50 years earlier. One third of children
are now born outside marriage, and although four-fifths
of births are registered by both parents there is no longer
a stigma attached to illegitimacy.[1] The majority of children live with both parents but one in five families is now
headed by a lone mother, with an increasing number of
children affected by divorce. Two out of three mothers
with dependent children are now working, but there is
a growing divide between families with two full-time
workers and those with none. Between 1979 and 1994
the number of children living in or below the poverty
line rose dramatically from one in ten to one in three,
including disproportionate numbers of children from
minority ethnic groups. Despite overall improvements in
children's education and health, inequalities persist. Rates
of illness, accidents and death continue to be far higher
for children from poorer homes, and even amongst those
who are well off there are increasingly high levels of
depression and mental health illness. For many families
living in inner city areas, particularly those from minority
ethnic groups and refugees and asylum seekers, life presents considerable challenges.

Over the past fifty years Coram has remained true to
its overall aim of giving children with the greatest levels
of need the best possible start in life, but has changed the
way it works in response to the changing circumstances
of children's and families' lives. The current work of the
organisation, now known as Coram Family, is covered
shortly but this chapter starts in the 1950s.

The Thomas Coram Foundation for Children, as the Foundling Hospital became known in 1953, was not alone in moving away from its original purpose, which was to remove children from their parents in order to give them a better life. As we have seen in Chapter VI, the Curtis Committee and the 1948 Children Act were strongly influenced by the work of the child psychiatrist John Bowlby at the Tavistock Clinic, who pointed to the crucial importance of strong and close early attachments between children and their parents as the basis for good mental health.[2] Children who are denied the consistent comfort, protection and care of a close and loving adult are likely to find it difficult to explore and play and experiment, and above all to form close and trusting relationships as they grow up. This pointed to the importance of supporting parents in the challenges of parenting, rather than removing children from their families.

Following the 1948 Children Act, childcare departments were established within local authorities, and children's charities such as Thomas Coram, Barnardo's and NCH began to appoint their own specialist childcare staff with social work qualifications to look at alternatives to residential care. Whilst most of the other children's charities continued to provide residential care, Thomas Coram moved from residential care to preventive work – supporting parents to keep their children rather than have them taken into the care of the State and, when this did not prove possible, on finding permanent families for children through fostering and, if possible, adoption.

The Thomas Coram Foundation was now a much smaller organisation than the Foundling Hospital had been. But with the appointment of specialist childcare staff the new Children's Department soon established itself as a leading children's childcare charity with a main focus on providing substitute family care for babies whose mothers were unable to care for them. Based at 40 Brunswick Square, in the administrative head quarters of the organisation and surrounded by its picture collection, for the next twenty-five years the Thomas Coram Foundation was largely a foster care agency – the only one of its kind.[3] Illegitimacy was still a social stigma and young single mothers who did not want their babies adopted had few alternatives in those days – there were no welfare benefits and no housing provision. Coram offered a unique service to those mothers.

'Moral welfare workers' and lady hospital almoners referred the 'unmarried mothers' as they were called to Coram, and the child care staff placed the baby in the residential nursery for a short time until the child could be matched with a foster family.[4] Once the babies were fostered, visits from birth mothers were arranged at regular intervals, and encouragement was given to the mother to make positive plans. A number of the mothers were later able to care for their babies, often when they married and their husband accepted the child. Others had the satisfaction of knowing that their children could remain safely and happily in their foster families, some of whom later adopted the children with the birth mother's blessing. These placements were referred to as 'either/or homes' – the foster parents being prepared to either foster or adopt. Delia Ashworth, the children's officer, pioneered a very high quality service that was well ahead of its time in providing substitute family care for children, with minimal disruption to the child and maximum involvement of the birth mothers.

In addition to these new foster children, Coram was also still responsible for the 500 children who were in the care of the organisation in 1955 when the residential arrangements ceased. Some of these children returned to their birth families or were able to live permanently with their foster families, but over the next eighteen years the Thomas Coram Foundation supported the foster placements of all of those remaining in its care. By the late 1970s some 500 children had been legally adopted from foster placements, even though Coram itself was not yet an adoption agency. It was also clear by the end of the 1970s that society's condemnatory attitude towards unmarried mothers was softening, and with the advent of the contraceptive pill it was also becoming easier to avoid unwanted pregnancies.

In the late 1970s Coram commissioned a study comparing a sample of these children placed with foster parents between 1948 and 1950 with a comparable group who had been placed directly for adoption by an adoption society. The outcomes for both groups of children were very positive, with the key ingredients of success being affection, commitment, optimism and a belief in the efficacy of family life. But those who had started as foster parents felt this approach was not ideal, due to the insecurity for both them and the child as they waited to see whether this would become a permanent relationship.[5] A further key finding, and one that lies behind much of Coram's

continuing success as an adoption agency, is the importance of ongoing support for foster and adoptive families.

Following the 1975 Children Act and 1976 Adoption
Act Coram has provided former pupils with similar
information to that now available to all adopted people
– their birth certificate and also a history of their parental background, prepared from the mother's confidential
papers by an experienced social worker. We saw in the
previous chapter how difficult it was for the children left
in the care of the Foundling Hospital to know who they
were when their names were changed on entry; or who
their parents were, as the governors promised the mothers when their children were accepted into the Hospital
that they would keep their names confidential. But it
was clear from the quotations from some of the former
pupils how damaging it was not to have a clear sense of
identity.

Nearly all the former pupils at the Old Coram
Association gathering had their own stories to tell of
their search for their birth families. A few of the older
pupils were fortunate that their mothers had responded
to Coram's initial tentative steps to find birth parents in
the 1950s. A number of mothers did agree to information being passed on, and some welcomed the contact
with their children. However many of these mothers had
not felt able to tell their husband and subsequent children about that first child:

> Former pupils often found themselves in the posi-
> tion of being a secret that could not be shared, and
> whose contact had to be passed off under some

other guise. One woman describes herself sitting with her mother's family, among brothers and sisters whom she felt looked like her, unable to speak about their connection.[6]

Some former pupils found that it was the birth of their own children that nudged them into deciding to visit the Coram social work team and ask for the information in their file. Others waited until they were into their seventies or eighties to follow up leads. In several cases it was the wife, husband, children or even grandchildren of former pupils who encouraged the first steps and perhaps even made the first tentative phone call. Some found a whole new and welcoming family, with brothers and sisters and nephews and nieces; some found coolness, or realised they were just too late; and some were rebuffed for a second time by birth mothers for whom the prospect of reunion was too painful.

Two participants in the research cited in the previous chapter describe the importance of finding where their mothers were buried. One describes a visit, accompanied by a newly found relative:

'So this is where your mother is buried.' We went down the rows and 'That's your Uncle George, and that's your grandfather and grandmother's grave.' And eventually I arrived at my mother's grave and … I made a complete circle really. It was the closest I've been to her – well, since she passed me on that day in 1912.

(Frederick, aged eighty-seven)[7]

Frederick had described his life before this as 'happy, but not complete', and that sense of completeness is echoed by Susan, aged eighty:

> … and when we found it [the burial place] oh we hugged each other and cried … Oh I've taken photographs and I sit and look at it sometimes, but it was like coming home to a family. Because I've gone to over 70 without thinking I've got anybody and all of a sudden … I mean I've started with nothing and I've got all these beautiful children … I just sit and look at all of them and there's a wonderful feeling.[8]

The service that Coram Family offers today to former pupils of the Foundling Hospital is described by Val Molloy, Coram's social worker responsible for this work.[9] The original petition or application to the governors is shared, together with the mother's name and the name she gave to her child. Sometimes details of the father are included – and 'what seems most important to former pupils is some sense of the nature of the relationship between father and mother'. But biographical details are only the beginning and as further information is pursued there is, for the first time, a sense of being connected to a past. Many of the personal accounts from the previous chapter explain, and demonstrate an understanding of, the reasons why their mothers were forced to pass their child over to the Foundling Hospital. Charles Nalden, for example, wrote 'My natural mother was now free to walk out of the Hospital gates to a fresh and unencumbered start in life … May God have blessed and protected her.'[10] Tom Erskine wrote:

> Though I never knew my mother, and have only very recently been made aware of the insurmountable difficulties she had to contend with at the time of my birth, I am eternally thankful to her memory and full of admiration for the way she, at much cost to herself, overcame the difficulties and made the much needed sacrifices to ensure my safety and future well-being.[11]

In 1971 Coram made the logical decision to become a registered adoption agency, offering a specialist service for children with special needs. Although many voluntary agencies today place children with special needs, in the early 1970s adoption was still seen as a service primarily for parents who were unable to have children rather than as a service for children who needed a caring family. The only children who were easy to adopt were those who were white and still babies. Older children, black children, and children with any form of learning difficulty or disability were unlikely to find an adoptive home. Over the past thirty-five years Coram's adoption service has led the way in setting up new approaches to adoption. The service not only places babies with medical and other special needs such as foetal alcohol syndrome, but also many older school-age children, sometimes sibling groups and children with physical disabilities.

Many of these children will have suffered neglect and abuse in the early months and years of life. The social

work team have developed specialist skills to assess potential adoptive parents. This is in order to ensure that such
children are placed in homes where the parents are suf-
ficiently resilient to cope with the inevitable challenges
that the children will throw at them once they feel
secure in the placement. This has led to two interesting
and relevant pieces of work at Coram. Firstly, a longitudinal research study of the development of attachments
between a group of 'hard to place' children who were
adopted between four and eight years old, which has
developed measures for assessing the attachments of both
adopters and adoptees.[12] Secondly, building on the insights
from this research, a very effective parenting skills training programme for use with adoptive families, based on
Webster-Stratton's *Incredible Years* parenting programme.[13]

A brief introduction to Mark conveys something of
the challenges and rewards of family life:

> Mark was placed with Debbie and Frank and their
> birth daughter Vanessa (aged 8) when he was three
> years old. His first eighteen months were spent with
> his young mother who was depressed and often
> neglected him or left him with different friends.
> He was fostered with three families before joining
> Debbie, Frank and Vanessa. He was a confused and
> upset little boy, whose language development was
> delayed. He easily collapsed into tempers and tan-
> trums. Debbie took six months off work to care for
> him and help him settle, and he did gradually calm
> down and become more trusting and affectionate.
> However he was sensitive to changes and jealous

of Vanessa, and she was upset at how much life had changed since he arrived.

When Debbie had to return to work she settled Mark with a childminder, and he gradually got used to the routine and then to the nursery. His concentration improved and he could join in simple games at circle time. In planning his move to school, Debbie and Frank arranged for an assessment and the education department have agreed that he will need a classroom assistant to give him one to one attention. At home he now has close relationships with all the family, and they have grown to understand his vulnerable areas and know how to support him at times of change. Without a family who could give him an enormous amount of individual care and stimulation it is likely that Mark would have dropped further and further behind other children. His lack of concentration and inability to cooperate with other children would have made it impossible for him to cope, and he could easily have dropped out of school.[14]

Other initiatives responded to new and emerging needs. The Coram HIV project began in 1994 to develop new models of substitute family care for children growing up in families where one or both parents had HIV/AIDS and might not live long enough to see the children through to independence. The project team worked sensitively and skilfully to develop creative solutions for children affected by HIV/AIDS that were acceptable to both their East African families and to social service departments, and made it possible for parents to retain responsibility and look after their children for as long as possible.[15]

The 'concurrent planning' project is another new approach, in many ways building on the earlier 'either/ or homes' approach in the 1960s when foster parents were often asked to adopt the children placed with them. Research showed that half of all children who came into care shortly after birth were still there at the age of four. Concurrent planning was set up as a response to both the negative effect of this drift and the delay in effective planning for young children. Launched in 1999, it built on an American scheme designed to speed up the process of decision making for very young children taken into care. The project works with local authorities to place with foster parents children who, at birth, are considered to be at risk because the parents have drug misuse or mental health problems, or difficulties in relating to or caring for their baby.

The Coram social workers work with the birth family to address the reasons for the child's removal into care, and at the same time facilitate contact between the birth family and their baby with a view to eventual rehabilitation. If rehabilitation does not appear possible within the nine-month time scale set by the courts, and if no extended family members are able to support the birth family, then the foster parents go on to adopt the baby. The child is therefore securely placed, and the risks (for the birth mother of losing her child, and for the adoptive family of not being able to adopt) are taken by the adults. The evaluation of the scheme showed particular benefits for the children, who moved more quickly to a permanent family home and experienced fewer moves between carers.[16] The experience can be somewhat of a roller-coaster ride for both the birth and the foster/adoptive parents. Jane Cambridge, a divorced woman in her mid-forties, describes the painful process of waiting for a child to be placed and the eventual placement of Sean, who she first fosters and then adopts. She concludes a long and moving article in *The Times*:

> I will gradually tell Sean the whole story about his background – how his 'tummy mummy' loved him so much that she fought to keep him, but that she was really too poorly to look after him – and how I had kept the name she had given him as a mark of respect for her. Each year we will have two 'contacts' with Briony [the birth mother], first in the form of exchanged letters and photographs, and secondly at a direct meeting, assuming that she is well enough. In the meantime we will enjoy Sean's childhood, secure in the knowledge that we are united for ever, mother and son.[17]

Sean has had a secure home from a few days old but will always know his birth mother. Briony knows that she will be able to keep in touch with him and watch him as he grows up, and Jane has a much longed-for child that she was able to adopt as a baby and can now love and care for as a permanent member of her family. The 'openness' of adoption may sometimes be challenging for the adoptive parents, but it does ensure that the adopted child knows and can value their birth family.[18]

The accounts of the former pupils who spent the whole of their childhood without knowing who they were or where they came from, and the impact that this had had on their self esteem, their sense of identity and their capacity to keep and form lasting relationships, has obviously influenced the way in which Coram now runs services for young people who have been in care. As the young people being fostered by Coram during the 1960s and 1970s grew up, the governors, under Peter Brown who chaired the Court of governors between 1975 and 1990, discussed how they could use some of the money they had invested to expand Coram's work. One of their first decisions was to use the skills and experience that had been developed over this period to provide more support to young people leaving care. In 1981 an Adolescent Project was established which, over time, became known as the Coram Leaving Care Service.

With the same emphasis on aftercare as the governors of the Foundling Hospital had always shown by keeping an eye on their apprentices until they were twenty-one, this service started with a specific focus on young people who had spent much of their lives in care being 'looked after' by local authorities and who, aged sixteen, were about to be left to fend for themselves. As any parent knows, the transition from adolescence to adulthood, and from school to college or employment, is difficult enough for those who have the benefit of a stable family life and supportive family to whom they can turn for help. But for young people leaving a children's home or other placement, the outside world can be a lonely and frightening place, particularly in large cities where housing is scarce and employment hard to find. Coram's work was based in houses which they bought or rented, and which offered bedsits for between four to six young people, with support from staff. It was hoped that the young people could learn to become self-sufficient, build up their self confidence, learn how to get along with others and gradually acquire the necessary skills to be able to attend college or seek employment. In addition groups were set up for young people with particular needs, for example, young mothers, or isolated and unemployed young men. The experience of Abu is typical of many of the young people supported by Coram:

Abu came to the supported housing in the Leaving Care service aged 17, having spent a large part of her life in care, due to sexual abuse and her mother's alcoholism. Her relationships with her family members were often very intense and difficult. Her mother's alcoholism was particularly painful and initially she had little contact with her father. Abu often had abusive relationships with men, and turned to drugs and alcohol to try to deal with the distress she felt. She recognised that she needed to love herself before she could establish positive relationships with others. She also struggled with her finances, particularly paying her rent and bills.

Her support worker in the Leaving Care service was able to help her work through her difficulties, worked with her on relationships and financial management, and encouraged her to go on a computer training course. This gave her purpose and stability in her life, and when she was offered a flat after 18 months with the service she felt able to move in and decorate and furnish it herself. She continues to keep in touch with her support worker.[19]

In recent years, new legislation such as the Children (Leaving Care) Act 2000 has required local authorities to take a more proactive role in supporting young people leaving care. Coram's service has evolved to include refugees, asylum seekers and other homeless young people amongst its clients. It has also provided a very successful education service for the young people, many of whom have had their education badly interrupted and have failed to achieve even the most basic levels of literacy and numeracy. These are young people who are likely to find it very hard to find and keep jobs, and include many who also have mental health and drug addiction problems.

The Coram team recently developed an accredited Life and Social Skills programme, including a manual and training package, that others can use with individual or group work settings with young people living in supported housing.[20]

The rise in homelessness in the capital in the 1980s was another area in which the governors felt Coram could make a difference. They therefore commissioned a review of families living in temporary bed and breakfast accommodation whilst waiting for permanent housing, believing these to be some of the most deprived children in London. The situation in which one borough 'received' the family but then placed it in another borough, which refused or did not have the resources to provide services, was not unlike that which Thomas Coram found with parishes under the Poor Law. The report found that the families were 'without ownership. They own very little themselves and are largely disowned by the support organisations.'[21] The families had considerable health, social, financial and housing needs but no-one considered that they were responsible for responding to this need. Perhaps most at risk were the babies born in the hotels who spent their first important two or three years cooped up in an overcrowded room and with inadequate food or play space. The report concluded that 'the plight of children growing up in inadequate and cramped hotel rooms in the 20th century should be as horrific to sensitive people as the children cast aside on dung heaps were to Thomas Coram'.[22]

The governors considered establishing a family centre linked to the existing children's centre but felt that it was not possible to expand this, given the long waiting lists and local catchment area. Instead, a Homeless Children's project was set up in 1988 which provided a range of peripatetic services to families living in temporary accommodation – toys and play activities, advice, counselling and information. The project reached hundreds of children in isolated and vulnerable families who were falling through the welfare net, helping to link families into statutory services, setting up groups and activities, and responding to individual need.[23] Despite its success, in 1993 the governors decided, largely for financial reasons, to close the project and the work was taken over by two other homeless families organisations based on Coram's campus.

For young people who have not had the benefit of supportive families, and who find themselves in and out of
care, it is all too easy to fall into a downward spiral which
may start with non-attendance or temporary exclusion
from school and gradually lead into petty crime and
homelessness. Poor attachments with their parents and
constantly being rejected or let down by adults can make
young people very angry and difficult. During the 1990s
it became clear that there was a shortage of provision
across London for adolescents with challenging behaviour. Coram responded in 1998 by setting up Fostering
New Links, a new approach to providing a home-based
therapeutic service for young people aged eleven to sixteen who might otherwise find themselves locked up in
secure accommodation.[24]

The service recruited a team of professional foster
carers, many of whom had psychiatric or social work
training, and who were paid social work salaries to provide twenty-four hour care for the young person in
their charge. Social workers and therapists supported
the placements and facilitated ongoing contact with
birth families, and teachers worked individually with
the young people in order to help them to return to
school and stay there. There was a huge demand for this
kind of service, and the young people referred posed
very high levels of risk of harm, both to themselves
and to others, with histories of abuse and neglect, and
mental health difficulties.

Sadly the complexities of running such a service,
which depended on a voluntary sector organisation
bringing many statutory agencies together, proved too

great. The costs became prohibitive and in 2004, despite the successful outcomes for many of the young people who had benefited from the placements, the governors once again had to make a decision to close an innovative service because it was not financially viable. Not for the first time, Coram had been ahead of its time for shortly after it was forced to close, the government began to fund a range of similar specialist 'treatment' fostering schemes which built on some of the lessons learned by Coram.

The evidence on the importance of continuing relationships between both parents and their children is compelling, even after family breakdown or when a child is looked after by the local authority because the birth parents are unable to do so. In the case of divorce it is very often the father who loses touch with his children if he is no longer living with the children's mother, and yet in the majority of cases it is in the best interests of both father and child to keep in touch. However there are difficulties if there are worries about possible abuse or abduction, or if the relationship between the parents is particularly acrimonious or there has been domestic violence. The Coram Child Contact service, set up in 1987, has pioneered a model for contact which provides a closely supervised and regular contact session in a neutral and homely venue for the visiting parent, and help for both the visiting and the resident parent on parenting issues. After skilled support, for a specific number of sessions, the parents are usually in a position to be able to manage their own antagonistic relationship better, and make their own arrangements for regular contact, which is likely to be much more satisfactory for the child.[25]

A similar service is offered to children who are separated from their parents by the courts, and who are being looked after by local authorities, and also for contact visits after adoption, as in the example of Briony and Sean.

This is the experience of Tariq, who now stays with his father overnight once a week and during the school holidays. His parents arrange this themselves but it wasn't always that way:

> Tariq's parents Anisa and Omar had an arranged marriage in Bangladesh but when he was three they separated after many difficulties including gambling debts and domestic violence. Anisa went into a Women's Refuge with Tariq.
>
> Tariq had not seen his father for nearly a year when he came to Coram Family. He saw him for over a year during 25 supervised contact visits. Omar was helped to accept his situation and deal with his anger so that he began to focus on Tariq's needs and understand his son's experience of being caught in the middle of parental conflict. It was evident from the beginning that Tariq loved his father and Anisa, seeing the blossoming relationship between them, was persuaded of Omar's commitment and genuine care for their son. Through careful work and then mediation, Tariq's parents were helped to arrange contact outside the centre. They reached agreement and when the case went to court an Order was not needed.[26]

One day in the High Court costs the public purse £5,000; Coram's successful work over one year with

Tariq's family cost just £1,760. For fifteen or more years Coram ran this unique service largely dependent on charitable contributions, but in 2002 the government were persuaded that this kind of service should be more widely available. Coram were then contracted to develop a training pack and to train the staff of centres to be established in each of the regions. The training and consultancy service is now a key part of this service.[27]

Most of these services are working with children who are separated from, or at risk of being separated from their birth families. But what had been happening on the old Foundling Hospital site for local children? When the fostering and adoption service returned to the Thomas Coram Foundation headquarters in 1955, the services for young local children and their families set up before the war were still being offered on the site between Brunswick and Mecklenburgh Squares, which is now known as the Coram Campus. The first of these had been St Leonards Nursery School, described in Chapter VI, which was evacuated to Hertfordshire during the war years. It was all hands to the pump after the war, as the newly appointed headmistress and her assistant mistress spent a whole term cleaning, painting and washing the nursery school in preparation for the children's return. The official opening ceremony was performed by the then Minister of Education, followed by a visit from Princess Margaret who was visiting Thomas Coram Foundation: 'the children were fearfully excited about this but very disappointed when they found that the Princess didn't wear a crown.'[28] The nursery school attracted long waiting lists, including children of many nationalities. It worked closely with parents and received referrals from hospitals and community doctors of children with special educational needs and disabilities.

By 1973, despite grants from the London County Council and then the Inner London Education Authority (ILEA), St Leonards Nursery School was finding it difficult to balance the books, particularly as the Thomas Coram Foundation was having its own financial difficulties. The Coram governors therefore proposed merging the nursery school and the day nursery into a single under-fives centre. This was not acceptable to St Leonards, and when Coram claimed back the premises, the nursery school governors decided they had no option but to close the school. The public outcry from parents and local residents was considerable, committees were formed, and eventually the ILEA took over two of the nurseries. What had started as a charitable endeavour had, after many successful years, become a State-supported school.

Meanwhile the Thomas Coram governors had their own plans, even if St Leonards did not wish to be part of them. During 1972/73 a working party had considered the future priorities of the Foundation and had decided, after taking the advice of Professor Jack Tizard of the Institute of Education, that a pre-school children's centre should be started to provide a comprehensive range of services for local children living in the catchment area of Brunswick Square, and building on Coram's day nursery. This was to be one of the first 'combined nursery centres'[29] following on from the establishment of Hillfields Centre in Coventry in 1972, and was in almost every way a forerunner of today's children's centres. The concept seemed obvious: combining nursery education and day care into a seamless service for the child and providing additional input from child health and social work, as well as support for parents through an integrated team of professionals from health, teaching and social work backgrounds. It was what parents were asking for. But in the 1970s it was an idea that proved to be way ahead of its time and the Coram Children's Centre which opened in 1974 under the leadership of Rita Marchant remained one of a very few until its eventual closure in 1991 and its reincarnation at the Thomas Coram Children's Centre a few years later.

   The brochure for the centre, published in 1976, has a very familiar ring today. The principles underpinning the centre were that education begins at birth and that education and care are closely interwoven – principles central to the government's pronouncements in 2004 on the development of a national network of children's centres.[30] Mother-child and father-child relationships are seen as important and to be fostered and supported at all times, and the nursery is to be closely integrated within its community – a modern philosophy, and one that is far removed from that of the Foundling Hospital. The new children's centre was open for fifty weeks of the year between 8.30–5.30 p.m. with places for seventy children including six children under two. The educational work of the centre was firmly child-centred and individualistic, with a strong emphasis on music and story telling, and records made on the progress of every child. A toy library and book library were opened in 1974, and there was a range of health services, including two paediatricians who held a weekly health clinic and regular visits from health visitors and speech therapists. The health visitor started a mother and baby group, but the parents decided to take it over and run it themselves as a playgroup.

There was a strong emphasis on staff training, and students from courses all over London had placements in the centre. The current head of a nursery school in Cornwall was one such student, whose experience at Coram in 1977 has had a lasting impact on her practice today. She recalls feeling that she was in a unique place, where children and staff were respected, where there was a commitment to providing the very best care and education for children with excellent opportunities for learning outdoors as well as in, and good food. The headmistress, Miss Marchant, gave strong leadership and guidance and emphasised the professional development of the staff – and cockroaches enjoyed the dressing-up baskets and story sessions as much as the children![31]

There were also good research links with the Thomas Coram Research Unit, part of the Institute of Education but so named because from 1973, under the direction of Professor Jack Tizard, it was based in the top floor of the children's centre building. Their research showed that in almost every respect this children's centre provided a model for what is now being rolled out nationally across the country through the Sure Start children's centres.[32]

The Coram Children's Centre provided a free, year-round, full day service for 100 local children, but when once again financial difficulties began to bite in the early 1990s, coupled with the discovery that the building was suffering from structural problems, the Coram governors decided they had to close the Centre. Again there was a vigorous local campaign led by parents, with a 1,500 signature petition to the Queen. Sadly the governors felt they had no option but to go ahead with the closure, but the parents' action was instrumental in setting up the Coram Community Nursery Association, a parent-run day care facility, partly funded by Thomas Coram Foundation, operating from a portacabin on the site. In the meantime St Leonard's Nursery School, by this time funded by the London Borough of Camden, continued to provide part-time nursery education for local children.

By the late 1990s the wheel was beginning to turn again. Another working party set up by the governors, under their new chairman Carolyn Steen, considered what future there might be for the site, and the concept of a Coram Community Campus was born. A successful bid to the government for regeneration funding under the Single Regeneration Budget (SRB) and the arrival of a new chief executive (the author) in 1997 with expertise in community development and early childhood education, led to proposals for establishment of a parents' centre, and for bringing together St Leonard's nursery with the parent-run community nursery as part of a bigger redesign of the campus as a whole. With the newly elected Labour government came the beginning of a remarkable period of expansion in early childhood services. One of their first initiatives was to promote the concept of 'early excellence centres', drawing heavily on the experience of nurseries such as the Coram Children's Centre some twenty-five years earlier. Coram was able to take advantage of the additional funding that this initiative brought and, in partnership with Camden Council and in response to the needs of the local community, established a new Thomas Coram Centre, comprising a 108-place nursery and a parents' centre on a newly refurbished campus.[33]

The Thomas Coram Centre drew on the earlier experiences of Coram but also on other research studies about the importance of high quality early learning experiences for children, and the role that parents play as their children's first educators. It has become a centre of excellence in every sense of the word, attracting visitors from all over the world, students studying for a range of different courses, and providing the base from which the Prime Minister Tony Blair launched Sure Start, a major national programme for parents and children under four, in 1998. The Parents' Centre has developed a whole range of services in its first ten years that respond to the needs of the local community including a drop-in centre; outreach work in schools and in homes; parenting education courses and programmes; a wide range of adult education courses; a music therapy service; an after school and holiday play scheme; specialist work with the Bangladeshi community; and a young parents project working with all the teenage parents in Camden and Islington. It has also been piloting the first accredited training course in the country for practitioners working with parents.[34]

The work with young parents is particularly interesting in its links back to the original Foundling Hospital. Many of the very young single women who make use of the support offered to themselves and their children might in earlier days have been forced to give up their children for good. Corinna Roberts was one such woman:

Corinna was brought up in a succession of children's homes from the age of two and a half. At nine, a foster family was found for her with her younger brother but by that time she was so angry with the world that she was sent back. Corinna emerged as a young adult with few formal qualifications and no experience at all of family life. Aged 25 she had her son Joshua. 'One thing I was adamant about was that no-one was going to take my child away.' Instead of taking Joshua away from Corinna, Coram Family has enabled her to become the best possible parent for him. Corinna started to bring Joshua to the parents' centre drop-in when he was six months old, learning to play with him. She became a regular. 'What kept me coming back was the way we were welcomed.' With no disgrace attached to being a single mother, and the recognition that however difficult the circumstances, it is almost always better for a baby to be brought up by his mother than in any other situation, Coram Family has become the maternal resource that Corinna never had, the place she has turned to at every point for help and advice.[35]

The Labour government elected in 1997 placed a very high priority on children and families in addition to the expansion of early childhood services. This was driven initially by a determination to reduce, and hopefully eliminate, child poverty (this led to an expansion in childcare to enable women to return to work), and to a determination to reduce social exclusion. Coram was able to take advantage a number of funding streams in order to develop new services – for example, initiatives such as Sure Start's local

programmes for parents with children under four, the
Children's Fund to support preventative work with children in the five to twelve age bracket, and Quality Protects
which brought support for children looked after by local
authorities. There has also been a strong policy focus on
consultation with and the participation of children and
young people. Coram has led the way here through its
Listening to Young Children project which has created a
resource pack for early years practitioners and parents on
how to see the world through the eyes of small children.[36]
The government subsequently paid for the training programme to run in every local authority in England.

But it was the death of eight year-old Victoria Climbié
in 2001, and the publication of a report which showed
how many opportunities to save her life had been missed
due to lack of co-ordination across agencies, that led
to the publication of a radical Green Paper *Every Child
Matters*[37] and the subsequent 2004 Children Act. With a
focus on improving outcomes for all children, and reducing the gap between those who do well and those who
do not, the new legislation requires a rethink of the way
that services are delivered so that they are more child
and family-centred, and very much more 'joined up'.
Children's Trusts are being developed in all local authorities to bring agencies together to plan and commission
services, and services are bringing together different
professions on the front line – in children's centres and
extended schools, for example. In many respects it reflects
the way that Coram Family has been working for years.

In addition to the ongoing work with children in
care, and the support for vulnerable children and families

in the locality of the Coram Community Campus, Coram Family's work programme in the early years of the twenty-first century has expanded to include services for vulnerable children and young people across the greater London area, as well as a number of family support services. All of these have at their heart the concept of resilience, helping children and young people to develop the capacity to bounce back when things get difficult for them, often by building up self-esteem and coping strategies. Over the past few years this has included the SkY-VoC programme in Southwark, working with children and young people in Southwark to help them overcome bullying and harassment; a number of projects based in schools, helping to reduce exclusions and improve educational attainment, and creating a closer relationship between parents and schools; and the boys2MEN project which works with vulnerable young black men who are at risk of moving into dangerous situations including crime, and at risk of not achieving their ambitions and losing opportunities for achievement. There has been particular interest in this project, which is expanding to meet the needs of boys and young men with significant emotional and behavioural difficulties. The range of family support services in London and Milton Keynes, include extensive use of the very successful Strengthening Families, Strengthening Communities parenting programme.

Before closing this account of the past fifty years of Thomas Coram's charity, we must return to the benevolence of the eighteenth-century artists and the historic treasures for which the Coram governors were responsible. By the early 1990s it was becoming clear that the art collection was in urgent need of conservation and that 40 Brunswick Square required expensive repair work. The building had been shut to the public for some years due to the risk of theft and the cost of insuring the art collection, and the governors were therefore faced with a dilemma. On the one hand here was an extraordinarily important collection of art to which the public had no access; but on the other it was not possible to use charitable childcare funds to keep it hanging on the walls. Counsel was consulted and ruled that it was outside Coram's charitable objects to set up a museum, and that if the governors wished to sell the pictures they must do so on the open market in order to achieve the best sale price for the charity. This would have led to splitting up the collection and a probable sale price some way below the actual value of the pictures if they remained as a collection.

The governors were reluctant to sell the pictures, after all they had been painted for and given to the Foundling Hospital. So, with the support of the Charity Commission, they agreed that Coram should create a separate charity (the Foundling Museum) and that the new charity should both run the museum and support the work of Coram. After meetings with the Heritage Lottery Fund, which had provisionally agreed a substantial grant to the Museum, it was agreed that the collection should be loaned to the Museum charity for a period of twenty-five years, during which time the museum would 'use all reasonable endeavours' to gradually raise the money to buy the collection from Coram Family, the proceeds going to Coram's work with children. At this point one of the Coram governors objected to the Attorney General that this was an unlawful transaction and the Attorney General agreed. A long series of discussions followed, including a debate in the House of Commons on 13 March 2001,[38] and eventually an agreement was reached. It had finally been accepted that the establishment of the Museum, with a requirement to gradually buy the pictures from Coram, was the best way forward. This decision was no doubt helped by the fact that expert advice had shown that the collection would be 50% more valuable by being kept together and put on public view.[39]

The Foundling Museum – in the eighteenth-century London's first public art gallery – re-opened in June 2004 to great critical acclaim. 40 Brunswick Square had been imaginatively turned into a space to show off its treasures to visitors of all ages. In addition to the original Court Room and Picture Gallery, beautifully restored to their former glory, the Museum includes a fascinating social history exhibition tracing the evolution of the Foundling Hospital, an education centre for children, an excellent café, and, on the top floor, the Gerald Coke Handel Collection which includes an exceptional Handel exhibition and study centre, where visitors can sink into a wing chair with a loudspeaker in the back and choose between opera and oratorio.

Handel, Hogarth and Coram would have been delighted to see how well their initial plans for using the arts to support innovative work with vulnerable children had survived the passing of the years.

LONDON'S FORGOTTEN CHILDREN: THEN AND NOW

The 265-year history of this unique children's char-ity – first the Foundling Hospital, then Thomas Coram Foundation for Children and now Coram Family – is inextricably bound up with the prevailing social and cultural mores of society over this period and chang-ing perceptions of childhood and children's place in society. Over this period there have been many occa-sions when Coram has led the way in developing new thinking about the care of children. This final chap-ter examines a number of themes that have emerged throughout the book.

In the eighteenth century children still tended to be seen as small adults, with little need of education, but of being some economic value to – or economic burden on – their parents. The emphasis, particularly for the poor, was on work in order that they should earn their way and make the minimum demand on the parish rates. Illegitimacy was thus seen as both an economic burden as well as a moral problem as a mother with a young child would be less well able to work. But this was still a period when only one in four children survived beyond the age of five, health care and education were minimal, and the only State support was through the Poor Law. The Foundling Hospital not only responded to the needs of illegitimate children and their mothers, but provided its children with considerably better healthcare and education than they would have found in the outside world.

The nineteenth century saw both a gradual growth in elementary education – not universally available until after 1870 – and the equally gradual introduction of laws to reduce child labour. The strong evangelical drive which led to the establishment of many other children's charities towards the end of the century was focussed on rescuing children from 'feckless' parents, saving their souls and educating them for their place in society. While the Foundling Hospital was never driven by the concept of soul saving, it did place a very strong emphasis on a useful education and proper preparation for a trade.

It was not until after the Second World War that the contribution of psychologists and psychiatrists to a better understanding of child development began to underline the importance of family life and of not separating children from their parents unless it was absolutely essential. The emergence of a welfare state which provided free education and healthcare and a safety net for poor families, together with this emphasis on family life, had a dramatic effect on the Foundling Hospital, and on childcare practice in general. The Foundling Hospital closed all of its residential provision in the 1950s, but children who are in the care of the State are still poorly provided for nationally, and much of the work of Coram Family today is with children and young people who have consistently been let down, both by their own families and by the statutory services.

The organisation that Thomas Coram founded and which the early governors set up and ran was remarkably innovative in a number of ways. There was no precedent for an organisation of this kind in the eighteenth century. Set up as a joint stock company dependent on voluntary subscriptions and donations, it was the world's first secular philanthropic corporation. Unlike Foundling Hospitals in other European countries, there was no support from or links into the established Church. From his relatively humble background, Coram succeeded in cajoling and persuading substantial numbers of the aristocracy and the newly rich merchant and professional classes to support his project, both financially and by serving as governors of the institution. Although it was only the men who joined the Court of governors it was their wives, sisters and mothers – 'ladies of quality and distinction' – who played a key role in raising the funds required, in providing moral support and in bringing an aura of respectability to the new charity. They were in many ways a forerunner of the 'ladies who lunch' who play such a valued fundraising role in today's charities.

Thomas Coram himself was also a force to be reckoned with. Tenacious and persuasive, a man of integrity, vision and commitment, he never gave up on his 'darling project' over the seventeen years that it took to come to fruition. From a modest background he was able to succeed against all the odds in enthusing sufficient people of standing in the country, and finally the King, to grant the charter that would enable him to set up the Foundling Hospital, even if his honest but somewhat intemperate manner led to the governors dismissing him from the general management committee sooner than he would have wished. A truly remarkable man, as can be seen in the famous Hogarth portrait.

The meticulous detail with which the governors planned and ran the Hospital lies behind both its success and its longevity. They were fortunate in attracting the support of several leading physicians who brought the latest thinking about children's health to the Hospital, or children's home as it would be called today. Amongst their suggestions were the importance of breastfeeding, which led to the practice of children spending their first years in the country with wet-nurses; the importance of an appropriate diet for the older children and an early argument about the links between diet and disease; a suggestion that all children should be inoculated against smallpox; and views about sufficient and appropriate clothing – care should be taken not to use too tight swaddling clothes as it would restrict the children's growth, and clothes should be changed on a regular basis.

The unsung heroes and heroines for well over 100 years were the local inspectors of wet-nurses, without whom the Hospital would have been unable to operate. They were responsible for all aspects of selecting and supervising the nurses and were instrumental in setting standards of care – critical to the welfare of the children. Until the nineteenth century they were unpaid. Many of them were women, possibly the first time that women had worked on equal terms with men in a national organisation.

The education that was provided in the Hospital may seem somewhat basic by today's standards but was a good deal better than that available to other poor children, and the music in particular gave many of the children a very special opportunity to enjoy singing, playing or just listening to fine music. The majority of the boys in the eighteenth century left the Hospital able to read, at a time when only 40% of the adult population could read, and the attention to the education of the girls was way ahead of its time. The care that went into planning placements for apprentices and the support that they were given until they were twenty-one was also beyond what one might have expected.

In her study of the Foundling Hospital in the eighteenth century, Maclure[1] summarised the philosophy of the organisation:

1 Work must always expand to the utmost that finances would permit.
2 Rehabilitation of the mother is almost as important as saving the life of her child. So confidentiality is key.
3 The organisation will take complete responsibility for all children until 21, or for life if they are handicapped.
4 Children and employees must be kept isolated from the contamination of the outside world.
5 The Foundling Hospital must show due respect for public opinion.

6 The standards of physical care, education, religious and moral instruction must be kept high, but suitable to the children's station in life (though the children were being educated above the level required to become servants and seamen, which reflect a gentleman's idea of how the poor should live).

7 There would be a willingness to experiment with new ways of doing things, but not change for the sake of it.

8 Children should be regarded as individuals and not numbers – they should be seen as a child of this hospital.

Compared to other poor children, or how their lives might have turned out had they stayed with their birth mothers, the foundlings were well cared for, reasonably well fed, secure and well educated. Their health care in particular was outstanding, provided free by some of London's top doctors, and with the exception of the period of open admission the infant mortality rate was considerably better than the national average. They would have been given both a system of moral values and a vocational training that would have prepared them for a useful working life. They were prepared for 'their station in life' which would have seemed entirely appropriate at that time. In retrospect, knowing what we know now about children's psychological development and the importance of close and trusting relationships between children and their care givers in the first months and years of life, the first five years spent with nurses and foster carers in the country would have given most children a secure and happy start to life. But the control, isolation and routine of the Hospital ill-prepared children for life in the outside world, and the shame and guilt of rejection and the 'sin' of their mothers would remain with them forever.

Many of the governors gave an extraordinary amount of time to the organisation. Most of the 375 governors who were named in the Royal Charter – mainly middle-class men of substance rather than aristocracy – had given money to the Hospital, and there were undoubtedly some who seldom darkened the doors of the Hospital again. But in the early days those on the General Committee met twice a week and oversaw the admission of every child, the appointment of all staff and every tiny item of expenditure. Although in modern times the rules have changed and governors' appointments are now time limited, up until quite recently several generations of some families have served on the Court of Governors over many, many years.

The key governor was the Treasurer, who lived in the Hospital whilst it was based in London. For most of the organisation's history the most senior member of paid staff was the Secretary and the governors played a very 'hands on' role in the running of the charity. Today, in line with modern practice and current charity law, the trustees of Coram Family (appointed by the governors) are still responsible for the overall direction of the organisation and ensuring that it is effectively and efficiently run, but the day to day management is undertaken by the chief executive and senior staff. Over the years the organisation has attracted many governors of distinction and, until very recently, has enjoyed active royal patronage. Amongst their number today are men and women with expertise in child welfare and some service users, but there are many others who come from very similar backgrounds to those in the early days – lawyers, accountants, business men and women and those with access to funding.

As is evident from Chapter VIII, the current Coram governors have had to make a number of difficult decisions over recent years and have had to close innovative and successful services where the costs of running the services have exceeded the funding available. They have also overseen the redevelopment of the Coram Campus and the establishment of the Foundling Museum as a separate charity, after a lengthy legal argument with the Attorney General which, had they lost, would have had serious implications for all charities with historic assets and not just Coram Family.

Another inspirational idea was to involve artists in the work of the Hospital. It was in many ways an act of 'enlightened self interest' (to quote the title of the Hogarth tercentenary exhibition), on the part of artists to accept the invitation to paint, donate and display their paintings of the walls of the Foundling Hospital, as there was nowhere else for them to show them to the London public. But the relationships that Thomas Coram developed with both William Hogarth and George Frideric Handel – all three of them childless but with a real commitment to improving the lot of children – was clearly fundamental to engaging so many of the greatest artists of the day in supporting the fledgling charity.

To design a building that was both appropriate for the 'charity children' and had rooms for smart fund-raising functions and a chapel that could provide the venue for concerts and Sunday services that would draw in the great and the good was a stroke of genius.

The modern Coram Family still attracts attention and support because of the pictures and treasures and the early history now on display at the new Foundling Museum. It also builds on the early tradition of annual concerts established by Handel by putting on Handel Birthday Concerts to raise funds for the charity every February. And the charity is the proud possessor of a huge modern painting, *The Coram Story*, which was painted by Rosa Branson to depict both Coram's history and its current work, and donated to Coram Family in 2002 (illustration 61).

Fund-raising is the greatest challenge that most voluntary organisations face and, throughout the history of the Foundling Hospital/Coram Family, the demands on the organisation have been greater than the resources available. Thomas Coram set up his organisation with donations, subscriptions and legacies sufficient to buy the land on which to build the Hospital and to care for up to 600 children, a relatively small number by comparison to the European Foundling Hospitals. In raising these donations he used the building itself and the paintings and music provided by the benefactors very effectively. It soon became evident, however, that there were many hundreds more babies being brought for admission than the organisation could cope with and the governors succeeded in obtaining a grant from parliament to support their work – conditional upon their taking in all children who were brought to the gates. The disastrous period of this 'general reception' is recorded in Chapter II. It led to the building of five new branch hospitals but to the death of huge numbers of babies. For a while the governors resisted the further demands of parliament to take actions which they thought would be detrimental to the children – for example, sending apprentices out at a younger age and charging a fee for them – but after four years the grant was terminated. However, two precedents had been created. It was the first time that government had seen itself as responsible for poor children, and had used a charity to channel support to them. And it was the first time that a charity had taken a grant from government and had experienced the lack of control over the quality of the work that so often comes with external funding.

At this point, faced with further financial demands and with donations beginning to dry up, the governors turned to property development as a source of income. They developed houses on the fifty-six acres of land that formed the Foundling Estate and raised considerable sums of money over the next 100 or more years from rental payments. Indeed, by the mid-nineteenth century the annual rental income equalled the original purchase price of the land. With the experience of the general reception fresh in their minds the governors resolved that it was better that a small number of orphans be kept well rather than a large number otherwise.

It was shortage of funds, together with the creeping urbanisation of London, that forced the governors to sell the Foundling Estate and move the children to Redhill and then Berkhamsted in the 1920s. And it was shortage of funds again that led the governors in the second half of the twentieth century to close down successful services. Raising sufficient income remains a challenge for Coram today. Most charities try to achieve a balance between voluntary income (donations and legacies), grants and contracts from central and local government, and investment income. Because of its reserves, Coram has in recent years appeared to be a wealthy charity and it has failed to raise sufficient voluntary income. This has meant that – like very many charities – it has not had sufficient freedom to develop and maintain the pioneering services that it wants to run, but has become very dependent on contracts with government, both central and local. Provided the services do still meet the needs of children and families this is not an issue, but the potential loss of independence is something that all charities have to guard against.

Throughout the eighteenth and nineteenth centuries the Foundling Hospital had to fend off criticism that, by providing a home for the illegitimate offspring of single women, it was encouraging licentiousness and wanton behaviour. There were clearly double standards at play here. Just as distinctions were made between the deserving and the undeserving poor in the debates around the Poor Law (hence the emphasis on work), so illegitimate births amongst the aristocracy were seen as unfortunate but acceptable, whilst support for the poor working class was seen as encouraging promiscuous sex. When Thomas Coram finally found the support he needed for the Hospital it chimed with a growing recognition of children as a national resource at a time when the wars against the French were requiring an increase in the population. He also succeeded in tapping into the growing commitment to philanthropy amongst the merchant and professional classes.

Although it was the sight of abandoned babies, or 'foundlings', dying on the streets that led Thomas Coram to seek his royal charter, from the beginning of the nineteenth century the charity was not a 'Foundling' Hospital at all, in as much as the term foundling suggests abandonment. Rather it was a home for illegitimate children whose mothers were forced to give them up to the Foundling Hospital because of the stigma of raising an illegitimate child. Children had of course been abandoned for thousands of years, usually because their parents could not afford to care for them, and not necessarily because they were illegitimate. Indeed, many children brought to the Foundling Hospital during the 'general reception' in the eighteenth century were legitimate.

But once the governors had changed the admission rules in 1801 there were two significant changes: the children were not abandoned, they were brought by their mothers who petitioned for a place in the Hospital; and their mothers were of equal interest to the governors, who sought to 'redeem' them by 'restoring them to a course of industry and virtue'. So from this point on, the charity was a home for illegitimate children, not abandoned children, orphans or foundlings. It is interesting that despite discussing a possible change of name on frequent occasions the governors did not actually change it until 1954, nearly 100 years after it was first mooted. Perhaps the continuing stigma associated with illegitimacy during the Evangelical nineteenth century was more than they felt potential donors could bear. The shame of illegitimacy continued until well into the twentieth century, as is clear from the accounts of former pupils in Chapter VII.

The story of the Foundling Hospital reflects the changing role of charities and their relationship with the State over the past 260 years. In many ways the Foundling Hospital set a pattern for charities and demonstrated just how effective a group of hard working volunteers could be. The way in which Thomas Coram set about creating a group of donors and supporters, and of engaging with artists to put on fund-raising events, also set the pattern for the way in which charities have subsequently built up their fund-raising strategies. The State played a very limited welfare role in the eighteenth century, providing some support for the poor through the Poor Law, but such education as was generally available was provided by either the private or the voluntary sectors or the Church, and the hospitals that were set up at about the same time as the Foundling Hospital were all paid for through public subscription. The role of the State was to fight wars (predominantly against the French) and uphold law and order. It was up to the charities – which mushroomed during the nineteenth century in particular – to lead the way and to develop services that, in time, the State often took on.

Today governments of all political persuasions see the voluntary sector as having a key role to play in providing services for children and families, and the sector itself has shown how well it can reach out to and work effectively with vulnerable and marginalised children, young people and families. Voluntary organisations like Coram Family can respond to the needs of children and families in innovative, flexible and unbureaucratic ways. They can take risks on behalf of children, and can focus on listening to and involving children and young people in the development of services. And they are not seen as stigmatising in the way that social service departments often are. But it is not easy for voluntary organisations to compete in the current 'contract culture', where the demands of competitive tendering are very considerable for small organisations and where competition with local authorities which do not have to include all their overheads in their costs can make the playing field seem very uneven. If the sector is to continue to play a part then new partnership arrangements will have to be hammered out, which respect the independence of the individual charities, whilst ensuring they have the capacity to develop new services.

Public attitudes towards children as small or inferior adults gradually changed during the eighteenth century, and for the first time they were seen as an important resource for the future of the country and therefore worth 'saving' and educating. Children in the Foundling Hospital were brought up to be healthy, well educated and know their place. But it was the focus on illegitimacy that marked out the organisation. The policy of enabling the mothers to return to gainful employment led to the secrecy over admissions and the changing of children's names that lasted well into the twentieth century. Unlike the children's charities that were set up at the end of the nineteenth century – NCH, Barnardo's, and the Children's Society – where the emphasis was on rescuing children from feckless parents, the Foundling Hospital remained focused on its dual purpose of bringing up illegitimate children and keeping faith with their mothers. But at a time when illegitimacy was still seen as a sin, the governors resisted all attempts by birth parents, foster parents or former pupils to change their policy of not letting children return to their parents. As Hannah Brown says in her account of life in the Hospital in the 1880s, children lost their mothers twice, once at birth and once when they left their foster parents, but the shame and humiliation were with them forever.[2]

It took the Coram governors some time to catch up with public and professional opinion that suggested that children were better off living in families or in small group homes than in large institutions, and the history of the organisation during the first half of the twentieth century, particularly when the children were based in Berkhamsted and the governors in London, shows just how out of touch they were. But in 1955, under the leadership of well qualified childcare professionals, Coram became the first children's charity to close its residential institution and to place all the children in its care either back with their birth mothers, or with foster parents or, in time, with adoptive families. Research into children's emotional needs, and particularly the work on early attachments between small children and their care givers, has informed Coram's work over the past fifty years. More recently, research from the field of neuro-science has suggested that the responsiveness of the parent or primary carer to their child, particularly during the first year of life, has a direct impact on the formation of the brain, particularly that part which regulates emotional responses such as empathy, self-restraint and the ability to pick up verbal cues.[3] Supporting parents during this important time with a young baby and supporting adoptive parents who have children placed with them are now central to the services that Coram Family provides.

Coram continues to develop innovative ways to foster resilience in vulnerable children and young people, helping to equip them with the skills and self confidence to be able to handle the many challenges of their lives. The experience of the foundlings is reflected in research studies which point to the importance of identity, of self esteem and of having a sense of control over the events of your life – of knowing who you are and feeling good about being yourself – as building blocks in resilience. One of the things that former pupils have found the most difficult is the secrecy surrounding their admission to the hospital and not knowing who they were or where they came from. Fortunately, there are few children for whom this is a reality today, but Coram Family works with many children and young people who have very low self-esteem because they have been rejected or abused or made to feel they are of no value. Building on the experience of the Foundling Hospital, one way of supporting children's emotional development is through the therapeutic use of music and the performing arts.

Another key factor is the presence of someone in your life – a parent, or a grandparent, or a teacher or care worker – who cares about what happens to you and is there to provide support when it is needed. This is where the aftercare of the governors in the early days played such an important role, as did some people in the Berkhamsted school who befriended many of the children who describe their time at Coram in Chapter VII. If children and young people have no experience of good relationships in their lives as children, then it is difficult to build relationships based on trust with their peers as they grow up, and much of Coram's work today responds to this.

Although an organisation with a national reach and reputation, most of Coram's services are delivered in London or areas within easy reach of London. There have been many debates about whether Coram should expand to deliver services across the country. The governors have come back again and again to the decision to work with a relatively small number of children well, to run high quality 'beacon' services that can be evaluated, and to use those lessons to influence policy and to support practitioners elsewhere through training and dissemination. This is evident through the brief summary of current work in Chapter VIII.

Much of Coram Family's work over the past fifty years has contributed to changes in policy at both national and local level. Since the mid-1990s there has been an unprecedented national policy focus on children and families. The government has funded a very considerable expansion in preschool services; has focused on the need for dramatic improvements in the life chances of children looked after by local authorities; and has recognised the importance of family life and of supporting families before they break down. These concerns came together in the *Every Child Matters* Green Paper and the 2004 Children Act, noted in Chapter eight. Coram has played a role in many of these policy discussions. Staff have contributed their expertise to changes to the adoption law and the competences and skills required of adoptive parents. Projects have explored new ways of working with troubled and troublesome young people, and improved contact arrangements for children not living with both their parents have been developed. The current focus on agencies working together to meet the needs of children and families; the considerable expansion of services for young children through Sure Start local programmes; early excellence centres; and, most recently, children's centres; the current recognition of the importance of both listening to children and young people; and of working alongside families if they are to give their children the best start in life – all of these took shape in Coram's services and projects.

It may seem a far cry from Thomas Coram's Foundling Hospital. But the pioneering spirit, the attention to high quality, the taking of risks on behalf of children, the importance of incorporating the arts and especially music into services, and the innovative approaches – all focusing on improving the life chances of very vulnerable children – are attributes that have survived for more than two and a half centuries.

Afterword 2022

A fourth reprint of this book some fifteen years after it was first published provides me with the opportunity to reference some more recent research into the Foundling Hospital archives, providing further insights into the running of the hospital and the experience of some of the 25,000 children who came into its care.

We can also explore how Coram, the continuing Foundling Hospital, has advanced the ground-breaking work begun by its founder and its pioneering work in early years and family support into a whole-child approach today; and how the Foundling Museum, established by Coram in 2004 to bring its historic assets to a wider public, has developed its role.

Revisiting the Past

Coram's historic archives, covering the years 1740 to 1954, provide a unique – and substantial – resource for researchers, covering some 800 linear feet of shelving or, as Berry[1] estimated, the equivalent of seventeen double decker busses. Coram is also the keeper of its modern archive, telling the story of the post-war development of children's services.

Recent detailed studies have thrown additional light on the very early years of the Foundling Hospital, from its opening in 1741 and through the years of the General Reception (1756–60), when a government grant required the governors to accept all children who were brought to the hospital. D.S. Allin,[2] after undertaking many years of painstaking analysis of the admission books, disposal books, inspection books, committee minutes and general correspondence, focuses particularly on the 15,000 children admitted during the four years of the General Reception. Including a detailed look at the role of the six branch hospitals set up to help manage the huge influx of children, he asks whether this period benefited the country in terms of lives saved or whether, given the high mortality rate, it did more harm than good. He examines the huge administrative burden on the governors of handling the reception of the children, the recruitment of 12,500 country nurses, the role of the 460 inspectors, the role of the branch hospitals, the return of the children to the Foundling Hospital and the apprenticeship of the 4,500 children who survived. Although the mortality rate during this period was in line with the national rate, and was only marginally greater than average for the hospital in other years, he concludes that, had the parishes sent pauper infants to country nurses (as became the law some years later), there would have been no need for the Foundling Hospital.

Further insights into the role of the inspectors and the workings of Barnet, the smallest branch hospital, are given in Tomlinson's research.[3] Prudence West, one of the hospital's many female volunteer inspectors, who went on to set up the small Barnet hospital, is described as hard working, determined and with a strong sense of duty, as she fought for what she thought was best for the young children in her care. The governors found her dogmatic and arrogant (few inspectors would have had the temerity to challenge governor directives) – but many of her charges thrived.

A spotlight is shone on the education and apprenticeship of foundlings during the first sixty years of the Foundling Hospital in Janette Bright's study.[4] The children were educated to know their place in society, and to ensure that they had sufficient skills to undertake and sustain an apprenticeship on leaving the hospital. The boys and girls were kept separate at play and at work, the boys learning to read, write and do basic accounts, and a range of practical skills that built up their strength. The girls were not taught to write during this period, but there was a strong emphasis on needlework (all the children mended their own clothes) and creating simple garments for sale to the public. Religious education was central to the moral education of all the children, as was singing in the chapel. Bright's analysis of the placement of all the children who were apprenticed during this period, of the jobs that they were required to do and of the steps taken to support those whose apprenticeships broke down, or who fell out with their masters, provides further evidence of the huge amount of detailed work undertaken by the treasurer (the senior paid official of the hospital) and the governors, and the detailed records that were retained that make for such rich reading today.

One of the most interesting studies to arise from the archives has been John Styles'[5] investigation into the small pieces of fabric which, for a short period, were pinned to the registration documents of each baby as they were admitted to the Foundling Hospital. The 5,000 small swatches of fabric dating from the mid-eighteenth century, many of them illustrated in *Threads of Feeling*, provided Styles with an unprecedented opportunity to investigate the dress of ordinary people of the Georgian period. More than forty different fabrics were found, some of them familiar today, for example, calico, flannel, gingham, tinsel, gauze and satin. Others were less so – camblet, fustian, susy, cherryderry, calimanco and linsey-woolsey, for example. Styles was surprised to find that nearly a third were printed cottons. While the aristocracy had patterns in silk, in the 1740s British manufacturers began to produce moderately priced fabrics stamped with flower and bird patterns. Even the poor were able to acquire pretty dresses, with a huge variety of designs. There were also many examples of embroidery, such as satin stitch, chain stitch, crewel work, patchwork and quilting. Sometimes a piece of the child's clothing might have been cut off to attach, such as a sleeve or a cap.

A third of the mothers attached ribbons, which would have added a touch of glamour to a plain dress and were also a symbol of romance and courtship. Many pieces of fabric conveyed messages (hearts, buds or acorns of hope) or were half of a piece of fabric, the other half retained by the mother in the hope of reclaiming her child. One such piece is half of a patchwork needle case embroidered with a heart, registered with foundling 16516. He was admitted in 1767, his mother keeping the other half of the patchwork, and was reclaimed in 1775.

Researchers have also been attracted to the tales of individual foundlings as traced through the archives. The 'hook' for historian Helen Berry's *Orphans of the Empire: The Fate of London's Foundlings* is the autobiography of George King (the only autobiography by a foundling in the early nineteenth century), who found himself 'caught at the front line of the struggle between Europe's great imperial nations'. Berry explores the early days of the Foundling Hospital, the world of work open to apprentices in the buoyant economy of Georgian London, the role of the governors in placing and supporting them, and the key role that the schoolmaster Robert Atchison plays in preparing George for life but also in providing a lifeline at times of trouble. George King, born in 1787, was originally apprenticed to a confectioner in London, but he ran away and in 1804 was press-ganged into the navy. His journeys took him to the Caribbean, Brazil and Argentina, and his memoir provides a humorous but harrowing account of life below deck, on shore and in the thick of battle. His vivid account includes the Battle of Trafalgar, where he fought aboard HMS *Polyphemus*, which took 200 French prisoners and towed HMS *Victory*, bearing Nelson's body, back to Gibraltar. Berry traces his final days to Greenwich Hospital, a charity for sailors falling on hard times, where he died aged 70.

Berry is not the first to conclude that the state has never been, is not and cannot be a good parent. But as this study shows, life in the Foundling Hospital did give some foundlings the resourcefulness, defiance and gritted determination to survive; and it did provide a base and somewhere to return to in times of trouble, where the foundlings' stories had a chance of being believed.

It is not just the archives that have brought us new insights into life in the Foundling Hospital. The pages of *Coram News*, the bi-annual magazine of the Old Coram Association (OCA), always include reminiscences of former pupils of their time in Berkhamsted, where the charity operated its residential school from 1935 to 1954, and often stories of the search for their birth mother. Books from former pupils such as that by Dorothy Soames' daughter Justine Cowan[6] continue to throw new light on this last period of admissions.

The OCA has continued to provide support for former pupils, as was evident in the opening pages of this book. The three gatherings a year – Coram Day in June, Charter Day in October and the Christmas carol service in December – have been a fixture in so many diaries for the past decades, providing a time to reminisce and renew friendships. As the number of former pupils still alive has dwindled, the committee decided that 2022 would be its final year, though Coram will continue to include news of former pupils in its own newsletters and to provide its ongoing support for them and their relatives in exploring their records.

The earlier days of the hospital have also caught the attention of novelists, such as Stacey Halls with *The Foundling*,[7] set in the 1740s. Two Foundling Museum Fellows have written popular books for children: Dame Jacqueline Wilson, one of the first such fellows, has informed a whole new generation of young people of the Coram story through her best-selling books about Hetty Feather, a young, red-haired girl left at the Foundling Hospital by her mother;[8] and so has Michael Morpurgo with his story of a friendship between Jonah and the foundling boy Nathaniel in *Lucky Button*.[9]

The Foundling Museum

The archives are also a rich source of material for the historic and contemporary exhibitions and commissions put on by the Foundling Museum. Two in particular have focused on the women in the Foundling Hospital story – the mothers who brought their babies and the women who supported and who worked in the hospital.

The Fallen Woman (2015) told the stories of the unmarried mothers who applied to have their babies admitted, with examples of petitions submitted by mothers to the governors. The mothers were interviewed (by an all-male panel) to try to convince the governors that they had been abandoned by the baby's father and, if the child was accepted, they would lead upright lives. They often had to produce character references from an employer or a doctor, and had their stories checked to determine those who could be rescued and those who the governors believed could not be saved. Both the petitions and a set of paintings, produced at the height of the Victorian age that were part of the exhibition, portrayed ordinary young mothers caught up in a terrible and unforgiving morality that meant abandoning their children in the hopes of securing a future.

Ladies of Quality and Distinction (2018) celebrated a centenary since female suffrage and brought together for the first time portraits of twenty-one of the duchesses and countesses who signed Thomas Coram's first petition to George II in 1735, helping to overcome moral concerns about the proposed hospital in persuading their husbands to support the petition. The exhibition also used documents from the Coram archives to explore the contribution of women who supported the day-to-day running of the hospital – the laundresses, scullery maids, cooks, infirmary nurses and school mistresses. A key figure was the head matron, who managed all female staff and the girls' wing of the school. As noted above, there were also the hundreds of countrywomen who were employed as wet nurses, and the inspectors who selected and supervised them, many of whom were women, such as Prudence West in Barnet. No women were appointed governors until the twentieth century, but gentlewomen and ladies of nobility offered advice and support.

Threads of Feeling and the autobiography of George King, both noted above, have informed excellent exhibitions. Others have included *Foundlings at War* (2014–15), looking at historic links with the military; *Treatment and Care of Disabled Children in the Foundling Hospital* (2016–17); and *Feeding the 400* (2016), looking at the foundlings' experience of food and the impact on their childhood and development – a rather more generous diet compared with most other public institutions.

There have also been exhibitions of music in the reign of George II, the Vauxhall Pleasure Gardens, on Charles

Dickens and John Brownlow, on his daughter the artist Emma Brownlow, and on Dr Richard Mead, the prominent physician who supported the Foundling Hospital in its early days and pioneered inoculation against smallpox and advocated for giving children fresh air.

An oral history project funded by the Heritage Lottery Fund enabled the museum to create *Foundling Voices* (2011) based on interviews with former pupils of the Foundling Hospital School. The exhibition was in five sections – early life, arrival, school life, out into the world, and search for birth families. It included reflections on the impact of illegitimacy, of the support of sharing with others through the OCA, the challenges over identity, and the emphasis on self-reliance and determination that they had to develop to get through life.

Foundling Portraits (2020–22) commemorated the lost faces of children given into care between 1741 and 1954, and included fine portraits of former pupils Lydia Carmichael, John Caldicott, Sylvia Copestake, Jocelyn Gamble, Henry Grainger, Pamela McMurtry and Ruth Miller, which are now hanging in the museum.

A number of exhibitions have explored the current experience of growing up in care, including work by Lemn Sissay on *Superman was a Foundling*, which has adorned the walls of the Foundling Museum since 2014. Inspired by Sissay, a popular recent exhibition, *Superheroes, Orphans and Origins: 125 Years in Comics* (2022), explored the life of foundlings, orphans, and foster and adopted children through the world of comics. *Flourish* (2006–07) showcased young artists who had been care, enabling them to express themselves and challenge preconceptions of the care system. The museum's pioneering creative programmes in early years with children on acute paediatric wards and with care-leavers attracted the patronage of HRH The Princess of Wales in 2019, and the museum frequently displays art made by the young participants, including graduates of its award-winning training programme for care-experienced young adults, *Tracing Our Tales*.

Since 2008, the museum has appointed Foundling Fellows, outstanding creative people who devise projects that celebrate its story and help deliver its mission to transform young lives through creative action. These have included Grayson Perry, Cornelia Parker, Yinka Shonibare, Lily Cole and Jackie Kay, as well as Wilson, Morpurgo and Sissay, noted above.

As Caro Howell, the museum director, wrote in 2014:

> The Foundling Museum is home to many amazing stories stretching back nearly 300 years: stories of heartbreak, hope, generosity, loss, resilience and imagination. Above all the stories we tell are personal. Whilst the Foundling Museum celebrates remarkable individuals like Thomas Coram, William Hogarth and George Fredric Handel, we also bear witness to those whose names or voices are lost to us, particularly those of the mothers and their children. The stories are not just historic, they are contemporary and urgent.

For further information on the work of the Foundling Museum, visit www.foundlingmuseum.org.uk.

Coram Today and Tomorrow

As Thomas Coram memorably said, 'I believe everyone ought in duty to do any good they can,' and the reach of the charity today exceeds anything that he might have imagined. The past fifteen years have seen the opening of new buildings on the Coram campus to accommodate the growing number of services provided by the charity, with a new reception and seminar area, the creation of the Pears Pavilion as a base for the creative therapies, and the Queen Elizabeth II building opened by HM the Queen in 2018 on the 350th anniversary of Coram's birth. Edward Newton, a former pupil aged 102 when he attended the opening, remembered a visit of King George V and Queen Mary when he was 10, and whilst HM the Queen noted in the visitors' book that she first visited the charity with her parents as a princess. To mark this anniversary, copies of Coram's own book, *Captain Coram, Champion for Children*,[10] were sent to every primary school in the UK, complemented by teaching resources at coramlifeeducation.org.uk and the book *Coram's Children*.[11]

As the first and longest continuing children's charity, Coram today is also the parent body of a specialist group of organisations reaching 1 million children, families and professionals each year and distinctive for addressing the whole child across family, legal, health and education systems, driving practice standards and policy impact.

Coram is one of the largest and most successful adoption agencies in the UK, consistently judged to be outstanding by Ofsted, and in 2022 the charity celebrated fifty years of Coram Adoption. The agency has continued to pioneer early permanence planning, ongoing support for adoptive parents and national matching services such as Adoption Activity Days, as well as being the first to deliver adoption services for local authorities. CoramBAAF, which joined Coram in 2015, is the UK's community of practice in fostering, adoption and kinship care, publishing a national journal and providing specialist support, advice and training for professionals from all local authority areas.

Getting young voices heard is at the heart of Coram's work today. Coram Voice (part of Coram since 2013), originally the Voice of the Child in Care, provides advocacy for children and young people in care and organises the only national 'Voices' writing competition for them. Coram undertakes extensive research into subjective wellbeing and experiences of children evaluating new approaches to inform policy and practice and developing its specialist Library of Care.

Providing legal advice to support the rights of children is the main focus of Coram Children's Legal Centre (since 2011), which brings forty years of experience in legal information, advice and advocacy, with its focus on the law and policy as they relate to children and young people. Recent work has included advice and outreach to address the challenges facing migrant or undocumented children, and this has also been the focus of much of the work of Coram International, which has worked with UNICEF and other agencies across the word.

Education, and particularly literacy and life skills, are brought to Coram through three organisations: Coram Life Education (since 2009), which reaches thousands of primary-school children through SCARF (Safety, Caring,

Achievement, Resilience and Friendship) online resource; Coram Beanstalk (since 2019), which trains volunteers to help children who are struggling to read; and Coram Shakespeare Schools Foundation (since 2020), which aims to build confidence and cultural capital through learning about and performing Shakespeare's plays.

Creative therapies are continuing to use music and art therapy with children and young adults who have experienced traumatic early life experiences, to help them build skills and emotional resilience.

Coram Family and Childcare (since 2018) provides a continuing focus on early years, childcare and support for parents, with its annual survey of childcare and work with Parent Champions.

In Coram today its story as the continuing Foundling Hospital lives on. *Voices Through Time: The Story of Care* is an exciting new initiative, supported by the National Lottery Heritage Fund, which has digitised 25% of the Coram archive. More than 1,000 volunteers worldwide have helped transcribe the digital images of these fragile records in preparation for online publication as part of the coramstory.org.uk website.

Young people who have experienced care have delivered a whole range of creative projects, including a spoken-word performance *What's in a Name*, a narrative blanket, installations and a public awareness campaign #RealStoriesofCare, reaching an audience of more than 6 million.

Coram has ambitious plans for the future, as it seeks funding for the Coram Institute for the Future of Children, the UK's leading centre dedicated to improving the life chances of children by bringing together research and development in children's care, seeking strategic solutions to specific problems, providing professional training and aiming to change hearts and minds for children through the Coram Story Centre.

As Coram Chief Executive Dr Carol Homden argues:

> 300 years after Thomas Coram established his charity, children's chances in life are still determined by where they live and who they live with as well as who they are. Every day Coram continues to create better chances that last a lifetime child by child and to address the future of our society by informing and inspiring the laws, systems and attitudes which can change the odds for the next generation. We shall not rest until every child has the best possible chance in life.

For further information on all that is summarised here see coram.org.uk.

NOTES

Introduction

1   The Foundling Hospital records are stored in the London
     Metropolitan Archives, where they take up 800 linear feet of
     shelving, comprising an estimated 8 tons of paper, and over
     1,000 plans. More recent files are kept at the headquarters of
     Coram Family.

Chapter I: Thomas Coram: The Man and his Mission

1   Jeremiah Dummer, Massachusetts, cited in Ruth McClure
     Coram's Children (Yale, 1981), p 19
2   Gillian Wagner *Thomas Coram, Gent* (Boydell, 2004), p 4. I am
     indebted to Gillian Wagner, a former chairman of governors
     of the Thomas Coram Foundation for the scholarship of her
     excellent biography of Thomas Coram
3   Letter from Thomas Coram to Revd Benjamin Colman in
     Boston. Quoted in Wagner, p 6
4   Roy Porter *London: a social history* (Hamish Hamilton, 1994), p 164
5   Daniel Defoe *Giving Alms No Charity, and Employing the Poor*
     London (1704)
6   See Jean Heywood *Children in Care: The development of services for*
     the deprived child (Routledge and Kegan Paul, 1959)

7   Maureen Waller *London in 1700: Scenes from London Life* (Hodder and Stoughton, 2000)

8   *The Guardian* 105 11 July 1713

9   John Brownlow *Memoranda, or Chronicle of the Foundling Hospital* (Sampson Low, 1847), p182

10 Jonas Hanway *Candid Historical Account* quoted in McClure's *Coram's Children*, p9

11 David Stansfield, alias CA *A Rejoinder to Mr Hanway's Reply to CA's Candid Remarks* 1760 quoted in Pinchbeck and Hewitt *Children in English Society. Vol 1. From Tudor Times to the Eighteenth Century*, p36

12 Roy Porter 'Every human want: the world of eighteenth-century charity' in *Enlightened Self-interest: The Foundling Hospital and Hogarth* (Thomas Coram Foundation for Children, 1997), p12

13 Society for the Propagation of Christian Knowledge

14 Thomas Bernard *An Account of the Foundling Hospital in London, for the Maintenance and Education of Exposed and Deserted Young Children* (London, 1799), p3, quoted in Wagner, p84

15 A full list of all the subscribers is given in Nichols and Wray's *History of the Foundling Hospital*, pp345–353

16 Herbert Compston, 'Thomas Coram, Churchman, Empire Builder and Philanthropist' (1918), pp98–9, quoted in Nichols and Wray's *The History of the Foundling Hospital*, p20

17 The relationship between Hogarth and the Foundling Hospital is explored further in Chapter four

18 London Metropolitan Archives A/FH/A03/002/001 General Committee Minutes, 4 March 1742

19 London Metropolitan Archives A/FH/A03/004/001/ Daily Committee Minutes, 25 March–22 June 1741, pp6–7

20 Wagner, p149

21 London Metropolitan Archives A/FH/A09/001 Billet Book 1741, March–May

22 Cited in Wagner, p188

23 When the Foundling Hospital was pulled down, Thomas Coram's coffin was moved to the vaults of the chapel at Berkamstead. It was later moved to St Andrews Holborn, where a copy of this inscription can be seen. The original inscription is still in the chapel of what is now called Ashlyns School in Berkamstead

24 Cited in Nichols and Wray, p14

Chapter II: The Foundling Hospital Gets Underway: The First Sixty Years

1   For this and other information I am indebted to R.H.Nichols
    and F.A.Wray *The History of the Foundling Hospital* (Oxford
    University Press, 1935); and Ruth McClure *Coram's Children:
    The London Foundling Hospital in the Eighteenth Century* (Yale
    University Press, 1981)

2   General Committee report cited in McClure, pp47–48

3   The records of all children admitted to the Foundling Hospital
    are kept in the London Metropolitan Archive

4   Nichols and Wray, p33

5   For a description of the role of the inspectors see Gill Clark
    *Correspondence of the Foundling Hospital Inspectors in Berkshire
    1757–6*, Berkshire Record Society vol 1 (1994)

6   Clark, p27

7   D. Owen *English Philanthropy 1660–1690* (Cambridge Mass, 1964)

8   J.A.Rouquet *The Present State of the Arts in England* (London, 1755)

9   E. Pollard 'A time for living: the story of Ackworth Hospital for
    exposed and deserted young children' *Friends Quarterly* 1960; and
    Nichols and Wray, p161–171

10 L. Hart *John Wilkes and the Foundling Hospital at Aylesbury 1759–
    1768*, p31

11 D.S.Alin *The Early Years of the Foundling Hospital* 1739/41–1773,
    www.foundlingmuseum.org.uk/collection

12 Jamila Gavin *Coram Boy* (Mammoth, 2000). See also the play of
    the same name adapted by Helen Edmundson for production by
    the National Theatre, 2005–2007

13 John Brownlow *Memoranda; or Chronicles of the Foundling Hospital,
    including Memoirs of Captain Coram* (1847)

14 Quoted in McClure *op cit*, p106

15 B.Young 'Rags to riches–the story of Paul Holton' in *The
    Wokingham Historian*, 9 August 1996, pp2–11

16 John Brownlow, pp189–190

17 A. Levene 'The estimation of mortality at the London Foundling
    Hospital 1741–99 *Population Studies* 59, 1, 87–97'

18 General Committee minutes, quoted in McClure, p143

19 Nichols and Wray, p223

20 Nichols and Wray, p265

21 McClure, p189

Chapter III: A Child's Eye View: The Early Days of the Foundling Hospital

1 General committee minutes, quoted in McClure, p190
2 Gill Clark 'Infant fashion in the eighteenth century: evidence from Foundlings nurses in Berkshire' *The Local Historian* February, 3–13
3 Quoted in McClure, p191
4 Dr Cadogan, quoted in Nichols and Wray, p129
5 Paper to the General Committee 29 March 1758 cited in Hart, pp17–19
6 P.M. Dunn 'Sir Hans Sloane (1660–1753) and the value of breast milk' *Archives of Disease in Childhood*, Neonatal Ed 85, 73–4
7 Quoted in Nichols and Wray, pp106–7
8 McClure, p212
9 See appendix VI in McClure, p270
10 McClure, p201
11 *Gentleman's Magazine* 17 June 1747 quoted in McClure, p193
12 Lord Chesterfield (1741) *Letters to his son*. Cited in Pinchbeck and Hewitt, p298
13 G. Chapman *A Treatise on Education with a Sketch of the Author's Method 1773*, quoted in McClure, pp119–220
14 Letter to Revd Colman 2 March 1737, quoted in McClure, p223
15 From *Psalms, Hymns and Anthems Used in the Chapel of the Hospital for the Maintenance and Education of Exposed and Deserted Young Children Foundling Hospital* (1774)
16 John Brownlow, p160
17 Quoted in Nichols and Wray, pp149–150

Chapter IV: Hogarth and Handel: Charity and the Arts

1 Quoted in David Solkin *Painting for Money: The visual arts and the public sphere in eighteenth century England* (Yale University Press, 1992), p158
2 For a full account of the paintings and other artefacts now on display in the Foundling Museum readers are referred to the Foundling Museum guide book, or better still are encouraged to visit the Museum to see the treasures for themselves
3 Jenny Uglow *Hogarth: A life and a world* (Faber and Faber, 1997), p333

4   Quoted in Wagner, p142
5   Brownlow, p12
6   Brian Allen 'Art and charity in Hogarth's England' in
    Enlightened Self-interest:The Foundling Hospital and Hogarth
    (Thomas Coram Foundation for Children, 1997)
7   George Vertue, cited in McClure, p67
8   Brian Allen, p11
9   For further information on the Court Room see Mike Bowles
    Tall oaks from little acorns grow (1997)
10 Cited in Brownlow, pp68–69. Brownlow includes a long
    description of the painting by Hogarth's friend Mr Justice Welsh
11 Brownlow, p15
12 John Orr and William Barnes *The Story of The Thomas Coram
    Foundation for Children and its Art Collection* (Thomas Coram
    Foundation, 1997)
13 Quoted in McClure, p69

Chapter V: No Goodnight Kiss: Brownlow, Dickens and the Nineteenth Century

1   William Wilberforce *A Practical Review of the Prevailing Religious
    System of Professed Christians in the Higher and Middle Classes in
    this Country, Contrasted with Real Christianity* (1797)
2   Readers might also enjoy *Tattycoram* by Audrey Thomas, a novel
    telling the story of the foundling Harriet Coram who goes to
    work for Charles Dickens
3   For a fuller discussion of the relationship between Dickens and
    the Foundling Hospital see Jenny Bourne Taylor '"Received, a
    Blank Child': John Brownlow, Charles Dickens and the London
    Foundling Hospital – Archives and Fictions' in *Nineteenth
    Century Literature* 56, 3, pp293–363
4. Quotations are taken from the article as cited in Nichols and
    Wray, pp285–291
5   Cited in Nichols and Wray, p307
6   A/FH/K02/051 General Committee Minutes Nov 1849–
    Oct 51 (microfilm X041/30) London Metropolitan Archives
7   Letterbook A/FH/06/002/011/:1849–53 London Metropolitan
    Archives
8   A/FH/K02/051 General Committee minutes Nov 1849–Oct 51
    (microfilm X041/30) London Metropolitan Archives

9   A/FH/06/002/011 Letterbooks 1849–53, London Metropolitan
    Archives
10 as above
11 A/FH/M01/029/01 John Brownlow's notes, London
    Metropolitan Archives
12 A/FH/K02/051–053 General Committee minutes (microfilm
    X041/030) London Metropolitan Archives
13 Nichols and Wray, p321
14 Nichols and Wray, p 318
15 Cited in McClure, p249
16 Cited in Nichols and Wray, p94
17 Cited in Nichols and Wray, p96
18 Wrottesley's *Report for the Charity Commissioners* 1840, A/FH/
    M01/014/01, London Metropolitan Archives. Some of this is
    cited in Nichols and Wray, p99
19 For a fuller account see Jenny Bourne Taylor, pp293–363
20 'English Charity' Quarterly Review 53 (1835) p499, cited in
    Bourne Taylor, p334
21 William Acton (1859) 'Observations on illegitimacy in the
    London Parishes of St Marylebone, St Pancras and St George;s
    Southwark, during the year 1857' Journal of the Statistical
    Society of London 22, cited in Bourne Taylor, p338
22 William Burke Ryan (1862) *Infanticide: Its law, prevalence, preven-
    tion and history* J Churchill cited in Bourne Taylor, p338
23 Brownlow
24 Bronwlow, p200
25 Cited in Roy Parker *Away from Home: A history of childcare*
    (Barnardo's, 1990)
26 See *Barnado's Children* (Barnardo's); Gillian Wagner *Barnardo*
    (1979); *A History of the Royal Philanthropic Society 1788–1988*,
    Rainer; Terry Philpot *NCH Action for Children: The story of
    Britain's foremost children's charity* (1994); John Stroud *Thirteen
    Penny Stamps: The story of the Church of England Children's Society
    (Waifs and Strays) from 1881 to the 1970s* (1971); Jean Heywood
    *Children in Care: The development of the service for the deprived
    child* (1959)
27 *Mundella report of the Committee into Poor Law Schools* (1896).
    Cited in Wagner (1979)
28 John Stroud
29 A Foundling *The Child She Bare* (date unknown – *c.* 1918)

Chapter VI: The End of an Era: The Foundling Hospital in the Twentieth Century

1   For a moving account of the 150,000 who were sent abroad from children's homes see Margaret Humphreys' *Empty Cradles* (1994)
2   Foundling Hospital *Annual Report and Accounts* 1918, p12
3   Foundling Hospital *Annual Report* 1919
4   Foundling Hospital *Annual Report* 1920, p22
6   Report on Scarlet Fever Outbreak, Dec 1921–Jan 1922, Foundling Hospital
7   General Committee minutes, quoted in Nichols and Wray, p324
8   Nichols and Wray p326. Coram's remains were moved to St Andrews Holborn in 1960
9   E. Hynes and S. Dennys *St Leonards Nursery School* (1974)
10 John Caldicott, personal communication, August 2006
11 John Orr and William Barnes, p17
12 *Report of the Care of Children Committee 1946*, HMSO Cmd 6922 The Curtis Committee
13 Curtis Committee Report op cit para477, p160
14 Letter from Miss Rosling of the Home Office to Colonel Nichols 12 February 1948
15 Letter from Col Nichols to Miss Rosling 3 March 1948
16 Ashlyn's School is now a grant maintained school, still on the same site in Berkamstead
17 Reported in *Coram News* Summer 1955, vol.9, no.1

Chapter VII: Who Am I? Where Did I Come From? Former Pupils Look Back on Their Childhood Experiences

1   Harold Tarrant interview for the Foundling Museum, 2004
2   For example Charles Nalden *Half and Half: The memories of a charity brat 1908–1989*; Tom Erskine *One of Coram's Children: The childhood and early adult life of a foundling in the nineteen thirties and forties* (unpublished); Bessie Vials' *Reflections: Short stories and poems* (1999)
3   Christine Oliver and Peter Aggleton *Coram's Children: Growing up in the care of the Foundling Hospital 1900–1955* (Coram Family, 2000), p17
4   Tom Erskine, pp15 and 19
5   Charles Nalden C. ch3

6   Christine Oliver and Peter Aggleston, p18
7   Christine Oliver and Peter Aggleton, p17
8   Christine Oliver and Peter Aggleton, p20
9   Charles Nalden, p87
10 Christine Oliver and Peter Aggleton *op cit,* p20
11 Kate Adie *Nobody's Child: Who are you when you don't know your past?* (2005), pp115–6
12 Christine Oliver and Peter Aggleton, p23
13 Tom Erskine, p30
14 John Caldicott, personal communication, August 2006
15 Virginia Makins interview with PI, June 2000
16 Christine Oliver and Peter Aggleton, p8
17 Val Southon, letter to *The Times* 21 June 2004
18 Sally Coombes in *Coram News* 43, 2, 1990
19 John Caldicott, personal communication, August 2006.
20 Interview with John Caldicott, Foundling Museum, 2004
21 Virginia Makins interview with PI, June 2000
22 Evelyn Siddons (2002) 'Open space. Reflections on institutional life', *Psychodynamic Practice* 8, 2, 229–235, p231
23 Interview with John Caldicott, Foundling Museum
24 Virginia Makins interview with LC, March 2001
25 Interview with Mary Bentley 2003, Foundling Museum
26 Bessie Vials interviewed in 'The lost children' by Rose Shepherd, *Saga Magazine* (March, 2004), pp90–94
27 Interview with John Caldicott, Foundling Museum 2004
28 Harold Tarrant 'The Foundling Hospital–within and beyond the gates' Lecture to the Friends of Thomas Coram, March 2000
29 James Rolstone (Jim Gravina) 'Fleeting thoughts on a summer's day' *Coram News* 50, 2, 1997
30 Cyril Ashby 'Recollections' *Coram News* 46, 1, 1992
31 Virginia Makins Interview with JC, 2000
32 Evelyn Siddons, p234
33 Interview with Mary Bentley, Foundling Museum 2004
34 Virginia Makins interview with DW, 2001
35 Interview with Mary Bentley, Foundling Museum 2004
36 C.M. Jeffreys in *Coram News* 39, 2, 1986
37 Interview by Alison Roberts in *Evening Standard* 9 June 2004
38 Val Molloy *Identity, past and present, in an historical child-care setting* (2002) p170

Chapter VIII: From Thomas Coram Foundation for Children to Coram Family 1955–2005

1   Gillian Pugh 'Parents under pressure: children and families, a view at the millennium' *Community Care* September i–viii 1999

2   See John Bowlby *Maternal Care and Mental Health* (Geneva, World Health Organisation 1951); John Bowlby *Childcare and the Growth of Love* (1953). For a further discussion see also Kate Cairns *Attachment, Trauma and Resilience: Therapeutic caring for children* (2002) and Helen Barrett *Attachment and the Perils of Parenting* (2006)

3   Jeanne Kaniuk '250 years of childcare at the Foundling Hospital' Lecture to the Friends of Thomas Coram 1998

4   For information on this period I am indebted to Dorothy Baulch, child care officer at the Thomas Coram Foundation between 1963 and 1983.

5   Lois Raynor *The Adopted Child Comes of Age* National Institute Social Services Library no.36 (1980)

6   See Val Molloy Identity, past and present, in an historical childcare setting (2002), p173

7   Christine Oliver and Peter Aggleton, p46

8   As above

9   Val Molloy, p174

10   Charles Nalden, p30

11   Tom Erskine, p4

12   Jeanne Kaniuk, Miriam Steele and Jill Hodges 'Report on a longitudinal research project, exploring the development of attachments between older, hard to place children and their adopters over the first two years of placement' *Adoption & Fostering* (2004), pp61–67

13   K. Henderson and Norma Sargent 'Developing the Incredible Years Webster-Stratton parenting skills training programme for use with adoptive families' *Adoption & Fostering* (2005), pp34–44

14   Coram Family *Annual Review* 200/01

15   For a description of this project see Jane Greenwood and others 'Positive outcomes for children and families: learning from the Coram HIV project Coram' (Family occasional paper 1, 1999)

16   Elizabeth Monck, J. Reynolds and Valerie Wigfall *The Role of Concurrent Planning: Making permanent placements for young children* (BAAF, 2003)

17 J. Cambridge, 'I never thought I'd be able to adopt' *The Times* 3 November, T2 pp 8–9, 2003

18 For a fuller discussion see Margaret Adcock, Jeanne Kaniuk and Richard White (eds) *Exploring Openness in Adoption* (Significant Publications, 1993)

19 Thomas Coram Foundation *Annual Review* 1997/98

20 *Life and Social Skills Manual* (Coram Family, 2005)

21 Valerie Howarth *Families in Bed and Breakfast Accommodation* (Thomas Coram Foundation, 1987), p5

22 Valerie Howarth, p23

23 Lonica Vanclay and Gordon Parker 'Reaching Out: Final evaluation report of the Coram Homeless Children's Project' (Thomas Coram Foundation for Children, 1994)

24 Lynn Brady, Judith Harwin, Gillian Pugh, Jane Scott and Ruth Sinclair *Specialist Fostering for Young People with Challenging Behaviour: Coram Family's Fostering New Links Project* (Coram Family, 2005)

25 Alan Slade 'Protection and supervision: making problematic contact safe and beneficial' in Argent, H. (ed.), *Staying Connected: Managing contact arrangements in adoption* (BAAF, 2002)

26 Coram Family *Annual Review* 2002/03

27 *A Guide to Best Practice in Supervised Child Contact* (Coram Family, 2002)

28 E. Hynes and S. Dennys (1974)

29 See Elsa Ferri and others *Combined Nursery Centres: New approaches to education and day care* (National Children's Bureau, 1981)

30 HM Treasury and Department for Education and Skills 'Choice for parents, the best start for children: a ten year strategy for childcare' (HM Treasury, 2004)

31 Personal communication from Janet Snook. Headteacher of Camborne Nursery School, Cornwall, June 2006.

32 For an evaluation of the centre see Martin Hughes, Berry Mayall, Peter Moss, Jane Perry, Pat Petrie and Gill Pinkerton *Nurseries Now: A fair deal for parents and children* (Penguin Books, 1980)

33 For further information on the developments at Coram see an early evaluation report – Valerie Wigfall and Peter Moss *More than the Sum of its Parts? A study of a multi-agency child care network* (NCB, 2001); Gillian Pugh 'Young children and their families: creating a

community response' (1999); and Gillian Pugh 'Children's centres and social inclusion' *Education Review* 17, 1, 23–29, 2003

34   For further information see Lucy Draper and Bernadette Duffy 'Working with Parents' in Pugh, G. (ed.), *Contemporary Issues in the Early Years*, 4th edition (Paul Chapman Sage, 2006)

35   Coram Family Annual Review 2003/04, taken from E. Crichton-Miller's 'Lost and found' *The Times* 12 June 2004

36   Y. Penny Lancaster and Vanessa Broadbent *Listening to Young Children Training pack* and CD Rom (Open University Press, 2003); and Y. Penny Lancaster *RAMPS: A framework for listening to children* (Day Care Trust, 2006)

37   '*Every Child Matters*' (Department for Education and Skills, 2003)

38   *Hansard*, 13 March 2001 column 171WH–194WH

39   For an account of the legal implications of this case see James Carleton and Judith Hill 'Thomas Coram and the Attorney-General' in *Christie's Bulletin*, Summer, 7, 1, 12–16, 2002

Chapter IX: London's Forgotten Children: Then and Now

1   Ruth Maclure *Coram's Children*, pp244–245

2   A. Foundling *The Child She Bare* (Swarthmore Press, *c.*1918)

3   See Sue Gerhardt *Why Love Matters* Brunner (Routledge, 2004)

Chapter X: Afterword 2022

1   Berry, Helen, *Orphans of Empire: The Fate of London's Foundlings* (Oxford University Press, 2019)

2   Allin, D.S., 'The Early Years of the Foundling Hospital 1739/41–1773 (Self-published, 2010, available on request from the Foundling Museum)

3   Tomlinson, Yvonne, 'Prudence West and the Foundling Hospital in Barnet 1751–71', in King, Steven and Gear, Gillian, *A Caring County: Social Welfare in Hertfordshire from 1600* (University of Hertfordshire Press, 2013)

4   Bright, Janette, 'Fashioning the Foundlings: Education, Instruction and Apprenticeship at the London Foundling Hospital, 1741–1800 (MA thesis, 2017)

5   Styles, John, *Threads of Feeling: The London Foundling Hospital's Textile Tokens, 1740–1770* (The Foundling Museum, 2010)

6   Cowan, Justine, *The Secret Life of Dorothy Soames: A Foundling's Story* (Virago Press, 2021)
7   Halls, Stacey, *The Foundling* (Manilla Press, 2020)
8   Wilson, Jacqueline, *Hetty Feather* (Corgi, Random House, 2009), plus five subsequent books
9   Morpurgo, Michael, *Lucky Button* (Walker Books, 2012)
10 Ollington, Robin and Wiseman, Albany, *Captain Coram, Champion for Children: My Story* (Coram, 2018)
11 Hatfield, Ruth, *Coram's Children* (Oxford University Press, 2022)

BIBLIOGRAPHY

A Foundling, *The Child She Bare* (Swarthmore Press, *c.*1918)

Acton, W., 'Observations on illegitimacy in the London parishes of St Marylebone, St Pancras and St George's Southwark, during the year 1857' (*Journal of the Statistical Society of London* 22, 1859)

Adcock, M., Kaniuk, J., and White, R. (eds), *Exploring Openness in Adoption* (Significant Publications, 1993)

Adie, K., *Nobody's Child: Who are you when you don't know your past?* (Hodder and Stoughton, 2005)

Allen, B., 'Art and charity in Hogarth's England' in *Enlightened Self Interest: The Foundling Hospital and Hogarth* (London: Thomas Coram Foundation for Children, 1997)

Allin, D.S., *The Early Years of the Foundling Hospital 1739/41–1773* (2010)

Barnardo's (nd) *Barnardo's Children*

Barrett, H., *Attachment and the Perils of Parenting* (National Family and Parenting Institute, 2006)

Bentley, M., Oral interview, Foundling Museum (2003)

Bernard, Thomas, *An Account of the Foundling Hospital in London, for the Maintenance and Education of Exposed and Deserted Young Children*, Second edition (London, 1799)

Berry, Helen, *Orphans of the Empire: The Fate of London's Foundlings* (Oxford University Press, 2019)

Bourne Taylor, J., '"Received, a Blank Child": John Brownlow, Charles Dickens and the London Foundling Hospital – Archives and Fictions' in *Nineteenth Century Literature* 56, 3, 293– 363 (2001)

Bowlby, J., *Maternal Care and Mental Health* (Geneva, World Health Organisation, 1951)

Bowlby, J., *Childcare and the Growth of Love* (Penguin Books, 1953)

Bowles, M., 'Tall oaks from little acorns grow' in *Enlightened Self Interest: The Foundling Hospital and Hogarth (*Thomas Coram Foundation for Children, 1997)

Brady, L., Harwin, J., Pugh, G., Scott, J., and Sinclair, R,. *Specialist Fostering for Young People with Challenging Behaviour: Coram's Fostering New Links Project* (London: Coram Family, 2005)

Bright, Janette, 'Fashioning the Foundlings: Education, Instruction and Apprenticeship at the London Foundling Hospital 1741–1800 (MA dissertation, 2017)

Brownlow, J., *Memoranda, or Chronicle of the Foundling Hospital* (London: Sampson Low, 1847)

Cairns, K., *Attachment, trauma and resilience: therapeutic caring for children* (London: BAAF, 2002)

Caldicott, J., Oral interview, Foundling Museum (2004)

Cambridge, J., 'I thought I'd never be able to adopt' *The Times* (3 November 2003)

Carleton, J., and Hill, J., 'Thomas Coram and the Attorney General' *Christie's Bulletin* Summer, 7, 1, 12–16 (2002)

Chapman, G., *A Treatise on Education with a Sketch of the Author's Method* (Edinburgh, 1773)

Clark, G. (ed.), *Correspondence of the Foundling Hospital Inspectors in Berkshire 1757–68* (Reading: Berkshire Record Society, 1994)

Clark, G., 'Infant fashion in the eighteenth century: evidence from Foundlings nurses in Berkshire' *The Local Historian*, February 3–13 (1999)

Compston, H.F.B., *Thomas Coram, Churchman, Empire Builder and Philanthropist* (London, 1918)

Coram Family, *A Guide to Best Practice in Supervised Child Contact* (London: Coram Family, 2002)

Coram Family, *Life and Social Skills Manual* (London: Coram Family, 2005)

Coram Family, *Annual Reviews 2000/01, 2002/03, 2003/04*

Coram News Twice-yearly magazine of the Old Coram Association (1955, 1986, 1990, 1992, 1997)

Cowan, J., *The Secret Life of Dorothy Soames: A Foundling's Story* (Virago, 2021)

Crichton-Miller, E., 'Lost and found' *The Times* 12 June 2004

Defoe, D., *Giving Alms Not Charity, and Employing the Poor* (London, 1704)

Department for Education and Skills, *Every Child Matters* (London: The Stationery Office, 2003)

Dickens, C., *The Adventures of Oliver Twist* (1837)

Dickens, C., 'Received, a Blank Child' in *Household Words*, 7 (1853)

Dickens, C., *Little Dorrit* (1857)

Dickens, C., and Collins, W., *No Thoroughfare* (1867)

Draper, L., and Duffy, B., 'Working with parents' in Pugh, G. (ed.), *Contemporary Issues in the Early Years* Fourth Edition (London: Paul Chapman Sage, 2006)

Dunn, P.M., 'Sir Hans Sloane (1660–1753) and the value of breast milk' *Archives of Disease in Childhood, Neonatal Ed* 85, 73–4 (2001)

Erskine, T. (nd), *One of Coram's Children: The childhood and early adult life of a foundling in the nineteen thirties and forties* (unpublished)

Ferri, E., et al, *Combined Nursery Centres: New approaches to education and day care* (London: National Children's Bureau, 1981)

Fielding, H., *The History of Tom Jones* (1749)

Foundling Hospital, *Psalms, Hymns and Anthems Used in the Chapel of the Hospital for the Maintenance and Education of Exposed and Deserted Young Children* (1774)

Foundling Hospital Annual Report and Accounts (1918, 1919, 1920)

Foundling Hospital, *Sermon Preached by the Rt Rev the Lord Bishop of Birmingham at the Annual Thanksgiving Service on 12th June 1921* (1921)

Gavin, J., *Coram Boy* (London: Mammoth, 2000)

Gerhardt, S., *Why Love Matters: How affection shapes a baby's brain* (Hove: Brunner-Routledge, 2004)

Greenwood, J.; Kaniuk, J.; Lindsay Smith; C.; Mwatsama, M.; Ndagire, B.; *Positive Outcomes for Children and Families: Learning from the Coram HIV project* (London: Coram Family, 1999)

Halls, Stacey, *The Foundling* (Manilla Press, 2020)

Hart, L., *John Wilkes and the Foundling Hospital at Aylesbury 1759–1768* (Aylesbury: HM&M Publishers, 1979)

Hatfield, Ruth, *Coram's Children* (Oxford University Press, 2022)

Henderson, K. and Sargent, N., 'Developing the *Incredible Years* Webster-Stratton parenting skills training programme for use with adoptive parents' *Adoption & Fostering* 29, 4, 34–44 (2005)

Hendrick, H., *Child Welfare: England 1872–1989* (Routledge and Kegan Paul, 1994)

Heywood, J., *Children in Care: The development of the service for the deprived child* (London: Routledge and Kegan Paul, 1959)

Howarth, V., *Families in bed and breakfast accommodation* (London: Thomas Coram Foundation, 1988)

Hughes, M., Mayall, B., Moss, P., Perry, J., Petrie, P., and
    Pinkerton, G., *Nurseries Now: A fair deal for parents and children*
    (Harmondsworth: Penguin Books, 1980)
Humphreys, M., *Empty Cradles* (Corgi Books, 1994)
Hynes, E., and Dennys, S., *St Leonards Nursery School* (unpub-
    lished, 1974)
Kaniuk, J., '250 years of childcare at the Foundling Hospital' Lecture
    to the Friends of Thomas Coram. (Unpublished, 1998)
Kaniuk, J., Steele, M., and Hodges, J., 'Exploring the development
    of attachments between older, hard-to-place children and their
    adopters' *Adoption & Fostering* 28, 2, 61–67 (2004)
Kingsley, C., *Water Babies* (1863)
Lancaster, Y.P., *RAMPS: A framework for listening to children* (London:
    Day Care Trust, 2006)
Lancaster, Y.P., and Broadbent, V., *Listening to Young Children* Training
    pack and CDRom (Maidenhead: Open University Press, 2003)
Levene, A., 'The estimation of mortality at the London Foundling
    Hospital 1741–99' *Population Studies* 59, 1, 87–97 (2005)
London Metropolitan Archives
    General Committee minutes A/FH/A03/004/001/25 March–
        22 June 1741
    Billet book A/FH/A09/001 March–May 1741
    General Committee minutes A/FH/K02/051 November 1849–
        October 1851
    Letterbook A/FH/06/002/011 1849 – 1853
    John Brownlow's notes A/FH/M01/029/01
McClure, R., *Coram's Children: The London Foundling Hospital in the
    Eighteenth Century* (London: Yale University Press, 1981)
Middleton, N., *When Family Failed: The treatment of children in the
    care of the community during the first half of the twentieth century*
    (London: Victor Gollancz, 1971)
Monck, E., Reynolds, J., and Wigfall, V., *The Role of Concurrent
    Planning: Making permanent placements for young children* (British
    Association for Adoption and Fostering, 2003)
Molloy, V., 'Identity, past and present, in an historical childcare set-
    ting' *Psychodynamic Practice* 8, 2, 163–178 (2002)
Morpurgo, Michael, *Lucky Button* (Walker Books, 2017)
Nalden, C., *Half and Half: The memories of a charity brat 1908–1989*
    (Wellington, New Zealand: Moana Press, 1989)
Nichols, R.H., and Wray, F.A., *History of the Foundling Hospital*
    (London: Oxford University Press, 1935)

Oliver, C., and Aggleton, P., *Coram's Children: Growing up in the care of the Foundling Hospital 1900–1955 (*London: Coram Family, 2000)

Ollington, Robin, *Captain Coram, Champion for Children: My Story* (Coram, 2018)

Orr, J., and Barnes, W., *The Story of the Thomas Coram Foundation for Children and its Art Collection (*London: Thomas Coram Foundation, 1997)

Owen, D., *English Philanthropy 1660–1960* (Cambridge Mass: Harvard University Press, 1964)

Parker, R., *Away from Home: A history of childcare* (Barkingside: Barnardo's, 1990)

Philpot, T., *NCH Action for Children: The story of Britain's foremost children's charity* (Oxford: Lion Publishing, 1994)

Pinchbeck, I., and Hewitt, M., *Children in English Society. Volume 1. From Tudor Times to the Eighteenth Century* (London: Routledge and Kegan Paul, 1969)

Pollard, E., 'A time for living: the story of Ackworth Hospital for exposed and deserted young children' *Friends Quarterly* (1960)

Porter, R., *London: A social history* (Hamish Hamilton, 1994)

Porter, R., 'Every human want: the world of eighteenth century charity' in *Enlightened Self Interest* , op cit (1997)

Pugh, G., 'Young Children and their families: creating a community response' in Abbott, A., and Moylett, H. (eds), *Early Education Transformed* (Falmer Press, 1999)

Pugh, G., 'Parents under Pressure: Children a families, a view at the millennium' *Community Care* 2–8 September, i–viii (1999)

Pugh, G., 'Children's centres and social inclusion' *Education Review* 17, 1, 23– 29 (2003)

Rainer (nd), *A History of the Royal Philanthropic Society 1788–1988*

Raynor, L., *The Adopted Child Comes of Age* National Institute Social Services Library no.36 (Allen and Unwin, 1980)

Report of the Care of Children Committee Cmd 6922. (The Curtis Committee, London: HMSO, 1946)

Rouquet, J.A., *The Present State of the Arts in England* (London, 1755)

Shepherd, R., 'The lost children' *Saga Magazine* March 90–94 (2004)

Siddons, E., 'Open space. Reflections on institutional life' in *Psychodynamic Practice,* 8, 2, 229–235 (2002)

Slade, A., 'Protection and supervision: making problematic contact safe and beneficial' in Argent, H. (ed.) *Staying Connected: Managing contact arrangements in adoption* (BAAF, 2002)

Solkin, D., *Painting for Money: The visual arts and the public sphere in eighteenth century England* (Yale University Press, 2002)

Stroud, J., *Thirteen Penny Stamps: The story of the Church of England Children's Society (Waifs and Strays) from 1881 to the 1970s* (London: Hodder and Stoughton, 1971)

Styles, John, *Threads of Feeling: The London Foundling Hospital's Textile Tokens, 1740–1770* (The Foundling Museum, 2010)

Tarrant, H., 'The Foundling Hospital – within and beyond the gates' Lecture to the Friends of Thomas Coram, March. (Unpublished, 2000)

Tarrant, H., Oral interview for the Foundling Museum (2004)

Thomas, A., *Tattycoram* (Goose Lane, Brunswick, 2005)

Thomas Coram Foundation for Children, *Enlightened Self-Interest: The Foundling Hospital and Hogarth* (London: Thomas Coram Foundation for Children, 1997)

Tomlinson, Yvonne, 'Prudence West and the Foundling Hospital in Barnet, 1757–71', in King, Steven and Gear, Gillian, *A Caring County: Social Welfare in Hertfordshire from 1600* (University of Hertfordshire Press, 2013)

Uglow, J., *Hogarth: A life and a world* (Faber and Faber, 1997)

Vanclay, L., and Parker, G., *Reaching Out: Final evaluation report of the Coram Homeless Children's* Project (Thomas Coram Foundation for Children, 1994)

Vials, B., *Reflections: Short stories and poems* (1999)

Wagner, G., *Thomas Coram, Gent* (Woodbridge: Boydell Press, 2004)

Wagner, G., *Barnardo* (Weidenfeld and Nicolson, 1979)

Waller M *London in 1700: Scenes from London life* (Hodder and Stoughton, 2000)

Wigfall V and Moss P *More than the Sum of its Parts? A study of a multi-agency child care network* (London: National Children's Bureau, 2001)

Wilberforce W *A Practical Review of the Prevailing Religious System of Professed Christians in the Higher and Middle Classes in this Country, Contrasted with Real Christianity* (London, 1797)

Wilson, Jacqueline, *Hetty Feather* (Corgi, Random House, 2009)

Wrottesley *Report for the Charity Commissioners* in A/FH/MO1/014/01 (1840)

Young B "Rags to riches – the story of Paul Holton' *The Wokingham Historian* 9, August, pp 2–11 (1996)

INDEX